DICTATORS

DICTATORS

by

JACQUES BAINVILLE

Translated from the French by

J. LEWIS MAY

KENNIKAT PRESS, INC./PORT WASHINGTON, N. Y.

DICTATORS

Published in 1937
Reissued in 1967 by Kennikat Press

Manufactured in the United States of America
Library of Congress Catalog Card No: 66-25896

Analyzed in the ESSAY AND GENERAL LITERATURE INDEX

CONTENTS

CONTENTS

THE PRESENT DAY

TO THE READER

DICTATORSHIPS are like a good many other things in this world. They can be the best, or the worst, form of government.

There are some excellent dictatorships, and there are some hateful ones.

Nevertheless, be they good or bad, it generally happens that they are imposed by circumstances, and, when this is the case, the people concerned have no choice but to put up with them.

Inasmuch as a nation cannot be too strongly urged not to drift into a situation which leaves it no alternative but helpless acquiescence, this brief and cursory survey of dictators as they have displayed themselves at successive stages of the world's history may not be without profit to the French people at this present juncture.

INTRODUCTION

WE are constantly deluding ourselves with the notion that things are new, when, in truth, we are but repeating the experiences of former generations and treading the paths which they long since have trod.

The dictatorships of our time came into being on the morrow of the day when President Wilson enjoined us to 'make the world safe for democracy'. The victory of the Allies was universally hailed as a triumph for the democratic spirit in all its varied forms. Amid the din of falling thrones, three empires came crashing to the ground. The monarchical system, by which the control of the State is vested in one sole person, seemed doomed to extinction. Who would have dreamt that one-man rule would ever come into its own again?

When the first dictator came upon the scene, his advent was greeted with incredulity. A few days, men prophesied, would surely set a term to his dominion. In France, one politician went the length of publicly deriding him as a comic-opera Caesar. And then, when the fashion seemed to be spreading, people consoled themselves with the belief that, if it was an epidemic, it would assuredly stop short at the frontiers of the Greater Powers, of those countries which had a liberal tradition at the back of them, and a firmly established progressive wing. As for inflation and debased currencies, these things, though not unknown, were looked upon as evils proper to im-poverished, primitive or ill-governed communities. It

9

was not for a moment to be thought of that the wealthier nations, equipped as they were with a well-organized financial system, would fall a prey to such grave disorders.

All this turned out to be a grievous miscalculation. The monetary system fell a victim to disease in the very places where it seemed to be flourishing most securely. Dictatorships sprang up in countries where they had long been looked upon as unimaginable. There they took firm root, despite the fact that, for a long time, the dictators themselves, when still no more than popular sedition-mongers, had never been taken seriously.

It is no mere caprice that has led us to connect a disordered currency with the emergence of despotic forms of government. The one precedes, and often begets, the other, because, for the vast majority of people, it is the most obvious symptom of national disintegration.

This, again, is one reason why dictatorships are not all assignable to a common cause. A dictatorship may be a defensive reaction against anarchy and ruin, and against the effects of democracy carried to its ultimate conclusion, that is to say, to socialism and communism. On the other hand, it offers to a democracy fired with equalitarian and anti-capitalist zeal, the means of overthrowing the forces arrayed against it, and of enthroning itself in their place.

There are thus many varieties of dictatorship. There are some to suit all tastes. Those who profess to abhor the very notion of a dictatorship would sometimes appear to adapt themselves quite tolerably to its conditions, and often, though they little suspect it, materially assist in bringing it about; while those, on the other hand, who pray most fervently for its advent, would often be sadly disillusioned if their prayers were answered.

But, alike for those who acclaim it and for those who abhor it, it is of vital importance to gain a knowledge of the divers phases it has assumed in the successive stages of the world's history, down to our own day, in countries at once so numerous and so remote from each other that it would surely be wrong to interpret as a passing fashion, a phenomenon which may be ascribed with far greater plausibility to the operation of a law, or to ineluctable necessity.

DICTATORS

THE ANCIENT WORLD:

GREECE
AND ITS 'TYRANTS'

GREECE, the mother of our civilization, knew everything, if she did not invent everything. To Greece we are wont to ascribe the glory of giving birth to the idea of republicanism. And rightly so. Nevertheless, it must be borne in mind that she countenanced dictatorships under the name of 'tyranny', a word which came in the course of time to assume an undesirable connotation.

For some hundreds of years, public life was non-existent in Greece. Peaceful guardians of their flocks and herds, its inhabitants were grouped in families under the authority of the sire, who was at once their leader and high-priest. The ancestral altar was the centre of their family life, and their religion the bond which united them.

It is impossible to state with accuracy the precise period when these families, comprising some hundreds of persons, actuated by a variety of influences of which the most cogent was the necessity of defending themselves against certain of their neighbours, gradually came to unite among themselves. The larger groups thus formed constituted the first tentative step in the direction of an organized social state, and was called a *phratry*. From the association of a number of phratries arose the *tribe*, and from the grouping together of several tribes, arose the *city*, a name which connoted, not only community of citizenship, but the actual place, more or less solidly constructed, which served them at once as a shelter, a general meeting place and a stronghold.

In the family, the supreme authority rested with the

sire. In the phratry, the heads of families, or patricians, wielded it in regular rotation, each of them, as his turn came round, offering sacrifice to the new gods, which had been adopted by common consent, and which were quite distinct from the household deities of each particular family.

The transformation of the phratries into tribes brought about an expansion of the religious idea, and the members of the phratries found themselves committed to the necessity of conceiving a new deity, more powerful than their household gods, a deity whose protection was to extend over the group as a whole.

There was no common bond between the members of the tribe, or, subsequently, of the city, save this community of religious belief.

The head of the family, the sire, still remained the ruler and the judge of his kinsfolk, and the sole repository of the right to dispense reward and punishment, a right which no one would have dreamed of contesting.

The government of the city was carried on by the heads of families, who assembled together in council whenever there was occasion to issue a decree affecting the community at large. Thus the government was aristocratic in character and derived its sanction from the religious idea.

It gradually became the custom for the patricians to delegate to the oldest member of their body, the right of offering sacrifice to the common divinity adopted by the tribes. Such was the first king. His authority, however, was exclusively confined to religious matters and did not extend to other questions. In everything that concerned the city, the concurrence of the heads of families was indispensable; the king was powerless to act without their consent, and whenever that consent was withheld, the king, having no means of enforcing his views, was obliged to give way. This arrangement lasted as long as the king consented to fall in with it.

It happened one day that a king arose who had a startling idea, and the courage to put it into force. That was to gather round himself, as their leader, all those elements in the city who had no family, phratry, or tribe to call their own: malcontents, vagabonds, aliens and the sons of aliens, that made up the *plebs*, who, being nought and confronted with the prospect of remaining nought, had a great desire to emerge from their nullity. By this means, the king in question endowed himself with an independent force, that is to say with a means of bringing pressure to bear on the tribes. He became, in fact, the first dictator.

He had many successors. The development of Greek society was marked by a series of revolutions, some of which were directed by the king against the aristocracy, some by the aristocracy against the royal power, and, finally, by the plebs, who looked on the monarchy as the main bulwark against oligarchical supremacy.

It was about the eighth century before the Christian era that the Greeks ceased to be a purely agricultural people. As a result of expeditions undertaken to divers places along the coasts of the Mediterranean, and of the trade and industry that thereafter began to flourish, their mode of life underwent a very considerable transformation. The reign of wealth was inaugurated. It brought with it a taste for commercial enterprise and inspired the more adventurous and intelligent section of the plebs, whom material prosperity was soon to convert into that intermediate social order we call the bourgeoisie, with hopes for their eventual emancipation.

This, the earliest manifestation of material progress, did not engender universal agreement. Far from it. In point of fact, the aristocratic party availed themselves of it, to the utmost limit which their predominance in the state permitted, in order to secure control of the main sources of revenue such as mines, forestry development, maritime works, export of cereals and cattle. But there also came into being an intelligent and industrious middle-class that contrived to derive substantial profit from the new order of things and felt it an intolerable hardship that they were allowed no share in the government of the country. Finally, the masses, while unwittingly reaping considerable advantage from this nascent capitalism, conceived a deep hatred of the wealthier classes, a hatred which diminishing respect for religion, hitherto so potent a factor in buttressing the authority of the patricians, largely served to exacerbate.

It was the plebs who furnished the earliest combatants in the class-warfare which, for century upon century, so cruelly rent asunder the city-states of Greece. That warfare was waged with unceasing and incredible ferocity. At Megara, where the social conflict had been as protracted as it had been sanguinary, Theognis, the bard, or rather the publicist, of the vanquished aristocracy, broke forth into bitter denunciation of those plebeians who, strangers but yesterday to law and order, had been wont 'to cover their nakedness with the skins of goats and to graze like stags without the city walls'. He longed, he said, to 'crush the brainless herd beneath his heel', and ended on a note of passionate execration. 'Ah!' he cried, 'Would that I might drink their blood!' And the two opposing parties did in fact drink each other's blood in the course of that long, unhallowed strife.

So fierce became the struggle that it was no uncommon occurrence for the all but exhausted opponents to agree among themselves to submit their quarrel to the arbitration of a third party, for fear lest the strife should end at last in their mutual and complete extermination. Invested with extraordinary authority, the peacemaker had all the forces of the government at his command, and retained them till his task was done. His work accomplished, and the state preserved from destruction, it only remained for him to go back to the obscurity of his private station. Here we may discern, so to speak, the dictator *in embryo*.

Sometimes, again, the opposing factions, feeling that a storm was brewing, anticipated the catastrophe by agreeing beforehand to refer the matter in dispute to some third party, revered for his virtue, his wisdom and his independence, on whom they called to draw up and promulgate a code of laws.

It is thus that we are brought face to face with half-mythical legislators like Lycurgus. From what we know of the famous Spartan lawgiver, we are disposed to think that he was a leader of the nationalist and communistic order. His black broth bears a significant resemblance to the millet of Moscow.

If he did not order the sterilization of the unfit, it was merely because he was ignorant of the method, inasmuch as he commanded that all puny and sickly infants should be put to death by drowning.

Greece also boasted a class of benevolent and legendary dictators. Among them was the famous Solon, whose memory, it must be confessed, seems to owe not a little to antiquity.

SOLON

AFTER the Megarians had been compelled by force of arms to abandon their claim to Salamis, a victory to which the Athenian populace had in no small measure contributed, the latter demanded that certain political rights should be granted them in recognition of the services they had rendered. At first the patricians seemed in no mood to accede to their request, but when distant rumblings announced that a storm was threatening, they grew alarmed and had recourse to the formula of settlement by mutual consent.

By common accord, Solon, who was held in the highest esteem, was entrusted with the task of reforming the constitution. His mode of handling the situation resembled that adopted by Gaston Doumergue after the 6th February.

With a like wisdom, Solon applied himself conscientiously to his task, remodelled the civil and criminal codes, sensibly ameliorated the condition of the poor, and satisfied no one. The poor he offended because of the privileges he had suffered the aristocracy to retain, the rich, because of the concessions he had granted to the common people.

Disappointed, but cautious, Solon embarked on a voyage and took ten years to complete it. As we should put it, he went back to Tournefeuille.[1]

[1]A small village near Toulon to which M. Doumergue retires after his period of office.

So this dictatorship, the earliest of which we have any detailed knowledge, ended in a deadlock, the dictator having been led, by inclination or necessity, to study the feelings of everyone.

There was now no alternative left but to try again, seeing that neither party was willing to renounce its determination to dominate the other.

PISISTRATUS AND THE
PISISTRATIDAE

THANKS to Pisistratus, it was the popular party that won the day. In him we have the first authentic example of a dictator placing his reliance on force and authority, and making use of them in the name of the people to combat the aristocracy. This new dictator had nothing in common with Solon. The prosperity of the body-politic had no interest for him, and it was by flattering the basest instincts of the multitude that he contrived to seize the reins of government.

Gathering around him a band of sturdy ruffians, he armed them with clubs and withdrew them to the Acropolis, thus gaining command of the city. He had carried out his 'March on Athens'.

In striking contrast to Solon, he made brute force the mainspring of his rule. *Tyranny* had now come into being.

To begin with, the word *tyrant* conveyed no opprobrious implication. It simply meant 'master'. A tyrant was the *leader*, chosen instead of the king, for in Greece, as in Rome, the ancient royal houses had been overthrown by the patricians, while it was the lower orders that had done their best to uphold them, and still vaguely deplored their disappearance.

It was owing to the propagandist activities of men-of-letters that the word tyrant acquired its odious significance and came at length to mean the unrestrained and

truculent exercise of individual power in complete disregard of the law.

The 'tyrants' invariably relied for support on the
lower orders. Never did any of them assume the leadership of an aristocratic movement. Their aims were
directed towards curtailing the privileges of the upper
classes for the benefit of the lower. Thus a tyranny,
which was to all intents and purposes a dictatorship
under another name, was the weapon of democracy,
while it was the aristocratic party that represented and
defended the cause of liberty. This evil and well-merited
reputation of theirs the class-war tyrants owed to the
great and wealthy, whose downfall they sought to bring
about. That they were 'levellers', who did not hesitate
to drag their opponents to the scaffold, is borne out by
a familiar story which has been told over and over again
in Greek and in Latin with divers variations. The Tyrant
of Corinth one day asked the Tyrant of Miletus to give
him some advice concerning the art of government.
The Tyrant of Miletus vouchsafed no answer but proceeded to strike off the ears of corn which had out-topped
their fellows.

Pisistratus ruled for thirty years, thanks to his army
of mercenaries, who were in reality precisely what the
blackshirts or the brownshirts are for Mussolini and
Hitler respectively. He ground down the upper classes
in order to defray the national expenses, which the wholesale distribution of gifts among the lower orders had
brought to a high figure. Religious festivals and popular
amusements occupied a considerable place in Athenian
public life. Foreign campaigns had brought about an

increase in the national territory, the people deemed they had been well served, and when Pisistratus came to die, they mourned his passing.

His two sons, Hipparchus and Hippias, succeeded him, but did not govern with their father's skill. Their adversaries took fresh heart. Certain youthful aristocrats set on foot a conspiracy which brought about the death of Hipparchus, who was struck down by Harmodius and Aristogiton. The illustrious heroes who thus struck a triumphant blow for Liberty and the Republic, and whose glorious deed has been celebrated in prose and verse by republicans, even to our own day, belonged in fact to the *jeunesse dorée*.

The dictatorship of the Pisistratidae had lasted fifty years. No sooner did it come to an end, than disorder broke out afresh. The plebs called attention to their existence by risings against the patricians. And so, proceeding from one *coup d'état* to another, Athens ultimately attained the goal of pure democracy. She was not destined long to remain there.

There was no truce to the struggle between the classes save when peril from without compelled the whole population of Athens temporarily to sink their differences in order to repel the barbarians. But as soon as the invader had withdrawn, strife broke out anew. No one then, was immune from the vengeance of the predominant party. Miltiades, the conqueror of Marathon, died in chains. Themistocles, the saviour of his country at Salamis, was condemned to death and had to seek safety in flight. The spectacle afforded by the Athenian democracy was not an exhilarating one. It had, in point of fact, always looked on a dictatorship as a weapon of social warfare, and on tyranny as an instrument peculiarly its own. Yet Greece was Greece, and wrought the miracle that only she could bring to pass — the miracle of Pericles and his rule.

PERICLES,
DICTATOR AND ARTIST

UNDER Pericles, social differences disappeared, with the exception, of course, of slavery. All Athenian citizens were equal in the eyes of the law, provided that they were indeed citizens of Athens. Their constitution, of which they were very proud, decreed absolute equality among them, and Thucydides affirms that it was merit, far rather than social rank, that opened the way to public distinction. No man, if he were capable of serving the city, was prevented from doing so by poverty, or the lowliness of his station.

Equality was the motive that underlay all social legislation. In theory, nothing could have been finer. Measures were taken to enable the poorer classes to exercise their civil rights. The State regarded itself as in duty bound to remedy, as far as in it lay, the evils arising from the unequal distribution of wealth, in such a manner, however, as to ensure that the benefits accruing to the needy should impose the minimum sacrifice on the rich. Public works, directed towards the adornment of the city and financed by the wealthy, gave employment to citizens who possessed no land of their own, or had not the means of enriching themselves by trade. Then, as the multitude must needs be kept amused, festivals and games were provided for them by the young folk of the well-to-do class who had the necessary time on their hands.

Such was the law, and we need not hesitate to describe it as an ideal law. Looked at from a distance it appears admirable. But its successful application demanded great political intelligence, address and flexibility on the part of the magistrates elected to administer it. The fact is that this splendid constitution was indebted for the smoothness of its working to a dictator well-nigh unique of his kind, a dictator who was also an artist and an exquisite, Pericles.

Nevertheless, he was no exception to the rule. He owed his rise to his alliance with the lower orders. Although himself of high lineage, he was not more than twenty-six when he put himself at the head of the popular party, to whose susceptibilities he pandered with unrivalled skill. His initial acts were directed towards crushing the opposition of the aristocracy. That done, he addressed himself to the task of governing the state, and his rule has left behind it on the map of history a track of unfading radiance. Possessed of the most brilliant intellectual gifts and the rarest political intelligence, he succeeded in conciliating the goodwill of the people, without ever yielding an inch in matters which he deemed essential to the welfare of the state.

So seductive were his gifts of oratory that a poet said of him, 'Persuasion dwells upon his lips'. Knowing the power he wielded over his hearers he never transcended the limits which the Greek people, sensitive beyond all others in matters of taste, were able to endure. Clarity of thought, poetry of expression, forceful dialectic, perfect integrity, absolute unselfishness, scorn of flattery, remarkable *finesse*, a profound knowledge of men, and a lively sentiment of the splendour of Athens and the greatness of her mission — such were the qualities which endeared him to his fellow-citizens, and enabled him to maintain his ascendancy for more than thirty years.

He was tactful enough to make the people think that they were governing themselves, whereas the truth was that the proposals laid before them had all been sedulously sifted beforehand and freed from anything calculated to revive the embers of bygone dissension.

Nevertheless, despite the wisdom of his rule, his later years were not unvisited by storms of popular discontent.

In spite of all the benefits he had bestowed upon them, the Athenians at last began to chafe at his control and lent a willing ear to demagogues whose aim it was to supplant him.

At length everything seemed to presage the imminence of his downfall. He was accused of making the democracy subservient to despotic rule; of shielding the champions of a philosophy which aimed at discrediting the ancient religion and — an argument well calculated to weigh with the multitude — of having diverted to State purposes money which ought to have been employed in bettering the condition of the people.

But so strongly was he entrenched, so conspicuous were the services he had rendered to the State, that his enemies dared not openly attack him. They chose rather to strike at him obliquely, through his friends.

Aspasia, his mistress, Phidias his friend, and Anaxagoras his life-long guide and counsellor, were calumniated, hounded down and haled before the court. Phidias died in prison, and Anaxagoras was compelled to flee.

Pericles' turn seemed about to follow when, in the very nick of time, a peril from without arose to save him. Not only did he make no effort to stave off the war with Sparta, he did his best to hurry it on, as affording the surest means of regaining all his old ascendancy.

And so it came about that, enlightened though he was, Pericles was reduced to having recourse to the most dangerous of diversions in order to maintain himself in power, to which he clung, not merely for his own personal satisfaction, but because he thought that he alone could rescue his country from the disruption which he saw approaching.

No sooner was war declared than he acted like a veritable dictator, suspending the constitution and imposing his will upon all, regardless of the protests which, the danger notwithstanding, were hurled at him from every side.

Victory would have set him up again. But defeat in the field, and, still more, the plague that now broke out and raged disastrously within the city, were his undoing.

For the plague, Pericles was not responsible. The utmost he could have been blamed for was that he had brought the dwellers in the surrounding country inside the city walls.

But the pretext sufficed. Pericles had been in power too long. The crowd, in which rich and poor were mingled pell-mell, insisted on a change at any price.

Put upon his trial, the dictator was mulcted in a substantial fine and nearly forfeited his life.

He died the following year, but not without the grim satisfaction of beholding the triumph of his military creed, and of being recalled to power by the very people who, but one short year before, had brought him to the ground.

Thus ended the most famous dictatorship of Ancient Greece, and one of the most noteworthy of all time.

Thanks to the matchless qualities of the dictator, it had borne the most splendid fruit; nevertheless, it ended in a war which was to involve the Athenian Empire in irretrievable disaster.

THE ANCIENT WORLD:

ROME

SUCH knowledge as we possess of the half-legendary times of early Roman history shows that the evolution of political power there was very similar to that of the city-states of Greece. The ancient royal house was overthrown by the nobles, and lamented by the people. Aristocratic in its constitution and traditions, the Senate was always apprehensive lest a man of the people should arise and make himself supreme.

The ancient Romans, however, being endowed with abundant practical wisdom, took care that, where the Republic had any weak points, the autocratic principle should be applied to reinforce them. Unlike the tyranny of the Greeks, which was always outside the law and always applied to the repression of one particular section of the community, the Roman dictatorship was sanctioned by law and carried on in the interests of the common weal. It was proclaimed whenever a grave peril, invasion, civil war or military revolt, menaced the safety of the *res publica*. Its duration was limited to six months, and its sole object was to enable the necessary measures to be taken for the preservation of public safety, regardless of any incidental hardships that such measures might inflict. Hence the famous motto, 'Let the public safety be the first law.'

A dictator, in the Roman Republic, was not chosen by lot, nor was he elected. He was invested with his powers by the Consuls whom he was intended to replace. The Senate, however, had the right to propose a candidate, and before long, this became their regular mode of appointment.

As long as his period of office lasted, the dictator's powers were absolute. He had complete control of every department of State, legal, military, administrative, executive. There was but one reservation, a financial one. For money, he was obliged to make application to the Senate.

On the other hand, in contrast with the practice at Athens, no accusation of any kind could be brought against him after he had laid down office and resumed his status as an ordinary citizen. Thus had the wisdom of Rome decreed, in order to ensure that his liberty to decide, and to act on his decisions, should be totally unfettered.

Such were the dictatorial functions with which Cincinnatus and Fabius Maximus, among others, were invested.

The office of dictator remained as long as Rome continued to be a military city *par excellence*, and as long as the Roman people maintained that warlike discipline which enabled them to vanquish and overcome their enemies, whether of Carthage or of the East.

But when the Roman arms had triumphed over their most formidable adversaries, the character of the people began to deteriorate. They fell into habits of luxury and self-indulgence, and superabundant riches, private ambitions and the mutual rivalries of victorious generals, each backed by an army that had come home laden with the laurels and the spoils of victory, gave rise to another form of dictatorship, the dictatorship of civil war.

The struggle for supremacy broke out and raged with the same violence, the same ferocity as in the cities of Greece. The old existing legal code was powerless to remedy this state of affairs and it may be said that it was precisely when the dictatorship disappeared as an institution *de jure* that it made its irregular *de facto* appearance in Rome. And so at last the Republic and its Senate passed away, and Emperors reigned in their stead.

Four names overshadow all others during the period of transition: Marius, Sulla, Pompey and Caesar.

MARIUS

GAIUS MARIUS, the son of humble parents, was a soldier of fortune. Having attained a rank analogous to that of a colonel in a modern army, he found that further promotion was denied him, as it was denied to all who had not filled one of the higher government offices. He therefore set to work to get himself elected tribune of the people. He achieved his object, thanks to the secret support of the patricians, who were at that time doing all they could to secure his advancement. They soon had reason to repent, thus affording the first example, but by no means the last, of conservative miscalculation.

His election opened out an illimitable field to his ambition. Having successively filled the offices of *aedile* and *praetor*, Marius was at length chosen to take command, under Metellus, of the army operating against Jugurtha in Africa.

Marius left Rome rejoicing in the opportunity that was now his of proving his capacity in war, which he hoped would bring him to the top of the ladder — to the Consulship. His hopes and expectations were abundantly fulfilled. He defeated Jugurtha and, despite the opposition of the aristocratic party, now thoroughly alarmed at his rapid rise to power, he was elected Consul.

Deeply incensed at the attempt that had been made to stem his progress, Marius flung himself into the arms of the popular party, who were gratified, but somewhat uneasy, at the eloquent general's already numerous changes of front.

The first reform which he carried out was highly democratic in character. It was to throw open the army to the plebeians and to give them the right to enlist for a period of sixteen years.

By this means he not only increased the fighting forces of the city, but provided himself with an army on whose loyalty to his person he knew he could rely. Here again we behold the system of the blackshirts and the brownshirts. The social outcast, the adventurer and the workless he provided, not only with a social position and the prestige of a soldier's uniform, but also with the assurance that they would never lack their daily bread, not to mention the prospect of costly booty.

Deeply read in the hearts and minds of men, he realized that he must give his soldiers a fresh symbol of solidarity and devotion. In place of the bundle of hay borne aloft on the point of a spear which, from time immemorial, had served as the military ensign of the Romans, but which had no longer power to fire the imagination of the younger generation, he gave them the eagle for a standard, even as Hitler hit upon the swastika. Then, his army equipped, trained, and sworn to his allegiance, he set sail for Africa, in order to settle accounts once for all with Jugurtha, who had again taken the field.

In less than a year, the Numidian King was a prisoner and his country completely pacified. Marius was now the idol of the Roman people. Consciously or unconsciously, Mussolini had the exploits of Marius in mind when he began to prepare for the conquest of Ethiopia.

The popularity of Marius was further increased when he defeated the hordes of the Teutones near Aix-en-Provence (*Aquae Sextiae*) and routed the Cimbri, who were threatening Rome itself. Contrary to law and custom, which required that an interval of ten years should elapse before a Consul could present himself for re-election, Marius filled the consular office five years in succession.

The venerable Senate, with its long aristocratic traditions, with whom he was not markedly popular, was disinclined to connive any further at this contravention of the law. They saw the danger, but they saw it too late. The battle began; the triumphant general carried the day and became Consul for the sixth time, owing his triumph to an alliance, which he effected for electioneering purposes, with the basest elements of the population.

From now onwards, Marius cast moderation and restraint to the winds. Laws were passed giving legal sanction in advance to the most arbitrary measures and proceedings. There was a law of *Lèse-majesté* for example, so vague in its provisions and so elastic in its object, that virtually anyone might have been arrested and put to death on the strength of it. Then came agrarian laws which allotted twenty-five hectares of the public lands to men who had completed their service in the Army. When all the public land had been distributed, private owners found themselves compelled to part with whatever portion of their estate a soldier might covet, though these acts of spoliation were not carried out without strenuous opposition on the part of the rightful owners.

In order to maintain an ever precarious popularity, he gave orders that the price of wheat should be lowered, and that the quantity of foodstuffs distributed gratis to the poor each month should be increased.

To consolidate his position, Marius set to work to obtain the Senate's sanction to his legislative measures. In this he was successful, and he would doubtless have established his personal authority on an unassailable basis, but that a fatal move on the part of one of his men enabled the Patricians to reform their front. They skilfully acted upon the feelings of the populace and upon the army, whom Marius had imprudently neglected. Deprived of their support, he failed to obtain his seventh Consulship and was compelled to quit the city.

The hour of the counter-revolution was now at hand. Marius beheld a new star rising above the horizon; the star of the man he looked upon as his most formidable rival: Lucius Cornelius Sulla.

Sulla, a youthful member of the aristocratic party, had been Marius's own Chief-of-Staff during the war in Numidia, a position which had brought him into prominence and had enabled him to ingratiate himself with the troops.

No less ambitious, and a great deal more sagacious, than Marius, Sulla had left his leader to play the demagogue alone. When he considered him sufficiently entangled, he broke with him and presented himself to the Senate as the champion of the patrician class whom Marius was striving his utmost to overthrow.

He rapidly attained the leadership of the senatorial party, and when the Italian tribes that were in revolt against Rome were preparing to take the city by storm, it was Sulla who was put in command of the army of defence. Inflicting the most terrible slaughter on the insurgents, he compelled them to submit. Thus the city was saved and Sulla was rewarded with the Consulship.

Returning to Rome, Marius furiously denounced him, and left no stone unturned to get himself appointed *generalissimo* of the army which was about to be sent against Mithridates, King of Pontus, a land of untold wealth.

The Senate hastily appointed Sulla; whereupon Marius, inciting the populace to revolt, persuaded them to veto the Senate's decree.

Sulla, whose army was already assembled, did not hesitate a moment. He ordered it to march on Rome.

This decision was a portentous one, for it had been expressly enacted, by a law which had hitherto never been transgressed, that no armed body of men should ever pass within the city gates.

The legions wavered. Sulla, realizing that hesitation meant ruin, lured them on with promises of booty, and prevailed on them to give battle to the troops of Marius. The latter were defeated, and once again the old general and demagogue was compelled to seek refuge in Africa.

Sulla now thought he had got rid of him for good. He re-invested the Senate with all its ancient prerogatives, procured the election of two consuls on whom he thought he could rely, L. C. Cinna and Octavius, and then set out for Asia.

When he was too far away for there to be any fear of his turning back, Marius returned to Italy, and, having secured the complicity of L. C. Cinna, marched with the forces he had rallied round him against the ungrateful city, which he attacked and took by storm.

At last the hour of vengeance for the demagogue dictator had sounded! The carnage was beyond description. For five successive days the slaughter went on. Patricians, senators, magistrates who could not, or would not, escape, were ruthlessly put to the sword, together with their wives and children. The streets ran with blood, what time the aged Marius was telling over with ghastly glee the severed heads of the senators and ordering them to be piled up on the tribune.

The aristocracy being thus completely crushed, Marius convoked an assembly of the people and, for the seventh time, was elected Consul.

His first act was to outlaw Sulla, and he was preparing to proceed to Asia to wrest from him the command of the army, when he fell sick and died, leaving the government in the hands of his son and the Consul Cinna, the same that had aided and abetted him in gratifying his lust for vengeance.

SULLA

AFTER the red terror, came the white.   Three years later, having conquered Mithridates, Sulla returned to Rome, bent on reprisals.   They in no way fell short of the massacres perpetrated by Marius, but, if one may so express it, they were more orderly.   Sulla, the senators' champion, was a stickler for form.   He caused himself to be legally invested with power to reform the constitution.   That formality having been complied with, the 'purge' commenced and was pursued methodically. Lists were drawn up and handed to various assassins, who proceeded to carry out their instructions in the victims' own homes.   Nor were these bravos recruited solely from the soldiery, or the common herd.   People of high social position, patricians, did not disdain to wreak their vengeance in person.   The famous Catiline, in particular, distinguished himself by the refinements of torture which he inflicted on his victims.

The work was paid for, so to speak, by the job, and the price of blood rose as high as two talents per head, that is to say to rather less than five hundred pounds of our money.   Thus there was no lack of volunteers.

From Rome the terror spread far and wide over the whole of Italy.   Every city known to entertain Marian sympathies was held to ransom, sacked, and its magistrates murdered in cold blood.

Having thus choked with blood, so to speak, all possibility of opposition, at least for some time to come,

44

Sulla provided Rome with a new constitution which deprived the plebs of the greater part of the rights they had so painfully acquired. The Senate, which Marius had reduced almost to the level of an advisory body, was accorded sovereign powers. The patricians breathed again and considered themselves assured of a long period of power.

However, Sulla's reforms were by no means so satisfactory as they had at first appeared. There was, in his autocratic system of government, no element of the stability required for adjusting the quarrels that were always going on between the plebs and the aristocracy.

The plebs might be terrorized into silence for the time being, but the day would surely come when they would seek to cast off the yoke that bore so heavily upon them. They had already tested their strength, and whenever a leader should arise and bid them cast down the oppressor, it was only too certain that they would obey his call.

Sulla's experiment was bound to end in disaster. No one can build a lasting social order on a foundation of blood, save by exterminating a whole race, and that is an impossibility. Perhaps Sulla's régime might have lasted longer if the dictator himself had lived, but he died two years after carrying out his counter-revolution.

POMPEY AND CAESAR,

OR THE DEFEAT OF THE REPUBLICAN ARISTOCRACY

I⊤ was no long time before Rome found herself threatened with a fresh outbreak of public disorder. Sulla being no more, the Senate was seized with panic and, having learnt from experience that nothing but force of arms could hold the plebs in awe, it called in the aid of a young general of twenty-six, named Gnaius Pompeius.

The precaution was wisely taken, for two disturbances soon broke out, the one aided and abetted by the Consul Lepidus, who had remained loyal to the memory of Marius, the other by Spartacus, who had incited the slaves to revolt.

Pompey vanquished them both, with the help of the Praetor, Marcus Licinius Crassus, who had turned general for the nonce. For a little while it was thought that the two saviours of their country, each with an army at his command, were about to fall upon each other, but they had the good sense to adjust their differences and to secure their simultaneous election to the consulship.

Henceforth, Rome had two masters, both of them mere politicians. No sooner were they securely in office, than these champions of public order found no more urgent work on hand than to betray the trust which the Senate had reposed in them and to pander to the ambitions of the common people, both being equally convinced, not only that Sulla's aristocratic system of government was out of date, but that it behoved them to look well to their own future.

Pompey had taken stock of the Senate's weakness and realized that, without an army to support it, it was incapable of effective action; whereas the people were free to act on their own initiative.

Premising, and very justly, that no government could regard itself as secure unless it could count on the unanimous support of the army and the people, Pompey used his best endeavours to bring those conditions to pass. And he succeeded.

He was now master of Rome; but, still unsatisfied, he thought to add further lustre to his name by some striking military achievement. He therefore set out for Asia where Mithridates, though defeated by Sulla, had succeeded in forming a fresh coalition.

When he returned to Rome laden with immense booty, he committed a capital error. He disbanded his army, ingenuously entertaining the belief that gratitude for the services he had rendered would be his sufficient guarantee. The Senate, seeing him thus defenceless, deemed the moment for revenge had come, and refused to grant him the honours of a triumph. There was no mistaking the significance of that decision. Ruin stared him in the face. Pompey realized his peril, and hurriedly sought the aid of the popular party.

It was now that he encountered Caesar.

In point of fact, he had known him long, but, being a very celebrated man and filled with the idea of his own importance, he had, when he deigned to notice him at all, looked but coldly and condescendingly upon the nephew of Marius, and that notwithstanding the brilliant manner in which the latter had discharged the tasks committed to him.

But Caesar had studied Pompey, and knew the weak spots in his character. He appealed to his vanity, and while drawing him on whither he wanted him to go, allowed him to fancy himself the leader. Thus it was that Caesar joined hands with Crassus, reconciled Crassus with Pompey, and persuaded them both that the three of them could share the world between them.

Thus was formed the Triumvirate which cast the existing Roman institutions on to the scrap-heap, and created an entirely new governing body. This, though nominally subordinate, was in reality nothing more or less than a dictatorship.

Caesar was at the head of it, and took for himself the proconsulship of Gaul, leaving Crassus to command the army that had been raised to wage war on the Parthians, while Pompey was to hold a watching brief on behalf of the partnership in Rome.

In order to win popular support for their measures, the Triumvirs had recourse to Marius's old plan. A law was passed assigning a grant of land to every citizen with three or more children to his credit.

Crassus and Caesar having taken their departure, Pompey soon revealed his incompetence. The political problems which had come to the fore in Rome since the departure of the armies proved wholly beyond his capacities. He could not even put down that dangerous firebrand Clodius who, although a man of no account whatever, was aiming at the highest office in the State.

If Clodius succeeded, it would be all over with the Triumvirs. Pompey, unable to make up his mind what line to take, made terms with the Senate and was appointed Consul, with the mission of delivering Rome from the terror which threatened it. Seeing this, and fearing stern measures of repression, the partizans of Clodius melted away, and, with them, disappeared the sedition they were fomenting.

Pompey imagined that the credit for this success was due entirely to him, and fancied himself strong enough to disregard the pact which bound him to Caesar. Crassus had already been removed from the scene, having met with a violent death in Parthia.

Being apprised of what was in the wind, Caesar made an offer to his *quondam* associate. Let them, he said, renew their alliance, or let them both lay down their office. Pompey refused, and prevailed on the Senate to order Caesar to disband his army before coming to give an account of himself in Rome.

Like Sulla before him, Caesar did not hesitate. He crossed the Rubicon, and marched on Rome. Neither Pompey nor the Senate had counted on that, and they fled into Greece. Caesar pursued them and destroyed their army at the battle of Pharsalia. That was the end of Pompey. He fled the field and soon afterwards fell by an assassin's dagger. It also marked the end of the Senatorial, that is to say the aristocratic, party.

Caesar was now able to return to Rome. He came back when he had pacified the regions that had suffered by the war, and was hailed with something like divine honours. He was appointed dictator and invested with legal powers far more comprehensive than any that had ever been held before him.

The Senate voluntarily surrendered its powers to the conqueror of Gaul. Once again the Republican aristocracy had to bow the head to a dictator. Caesarism was born. By one of those misapprehensions which so plentifully strew the path of history and of politics, the word has come to be a synonym for reaction, whereas the fact is that Caesarism was rigidly opposed to the old institutions, to the patrician class and the conservatives.

Feeling his position secure, Caesar set himself to reform the State on a great scale. Reforms of the judicial system, social legislation, statutes affecting slaves and regulating their employment, sumptuary laws to limit and control the display of wealth and luxury —all these followed one after another, in quick succession. The whole thing was pretty definitely Fascist and explains Mussolini's worship of the 'divine Julius'.

But there was one thing above all others that was Caesar's crowning glory; one thing that has made his name immortal. He always rose above the level of mere party considerations. Like Pericles at Athens, he had but one thing at heart, the glory and the greatness of his country.

His political insight enabled him to understand that, after being torn asunder by so many years of civil strife, the thing the country longed for beyond all others was peace. This he hastened to bring about by means of generous amnesties, by being the first to set the example of forgiveness of wrongs done, bestowing missions and offices on the very men who in the past had been his bitterest opponents.

At last after seventy years of conspiracies, insurrection and wholesale slaughter, Rome was able to breathe again, and the awe in which Caesar was held enabled him to keep the democracy in order when he had finished making use of it to gain the supreme power for himself. The plebs, now kept well in hand, were compelled to abandon their idle ways. The number of persons on the dole was cut down by more than a half. At no more than twenty four hours' notice, two hundred thousand Romans found themselves obliged to provide for their own subsistence, and, as the colonies were in need of labour, they were offered a free passage to go out and work on the land. It was in this way that southern Gaul and northern Africa were colonized. Rome felt the grip of a strong will.

Social order was re-established. The Dictator began to make ready to carry out, once for all, the pacification of the Eastern provinces, where smouldering fires of discontent broke ever and anon into flames of open rebellion.

But a conspiracy against his life left Caesar no time to complete his task. A certain group of patricians had made up their minds to kill him, and fearing lest their attempt might miscarry if they attacked him in public, they decided to strike at him within the precincts of that Senate which he had so profoundly transformed, and whose powers he had so ruthlessly curtailed. Their deed, they reflected, would thus acquire a more impressive significance. The plot was carefully laid, and it succeeded. On the 15th March, in the year 44 B.C., Caesar fell, stabbed to death with twenty-three wounds in his body. Brutus, to this day, is looked on as a hero and a martyr of the Republic. That is only true if we add that the Republic in question was in fact an oligarchy, very much like the 'two hundred families' that M. Léon Blum and the *Front populaire* make the object of their daily denunciations, the main difference being that in Rome the families could be named.

However, the conspirators had banked on a chimera. The day of Caesar's burial, Antony, the victim's chief lieutenant, stirred up the people against the assassins, who were compelled to flee. Their fellow members in the Senate, whose movements were strictly shadowed, hastily disavowed them.

For a time it looked as if the old troubles would break out again. But Caesar had not laboured in vain. From all parts of the Empire there rose up a passionate longing for peace and stable rule, little calculated to encourage the partisans of republican liberty and senatorial government. And so, when the dead man's adopted son arrived in Rome, he was hailed as his rightful heir.

Nevertheless, Octavius was obliged to share the government with Antony, who had seized the public funds, and with Lepidus, who still enjoyed a certain measure of popularity with the army. This was the Triumvirate over again. It was tolerated as a transitional and temporary expedient. Some further sporadic outbreaks there were fated to be, but the Roman world as a whole demanded the cessation of party strife. The age of major conflicts was over. A final insurrection flared up but it was soon extinguished. And Octavius Caesar, with no Antony to hinder him, stood forth as the sole master of Rome, and of the world.

The Republic was dead.

A hundred years of disorder, riots, conspiracies, revolutions, massacres, such as the world had never known, culminated in the establishment of an absolute monarchy and the upshot of it all was that the people, who had always lamented the passing of the earlier kings, descendants of Romulus and Remus, those heroes old in story, had at last brought the aristocracy to its knees.

MODERN TIMES

CROMWELL, LORD PROTECTOR

BETWEEN antiquity and modern times, the idea of dictatorship seems to have been non-existent. Of the idea, as of the thing itself, we find no trace. The Middle Ages disappear in a sort of mediaeval pageant. Why is this? First and foremost because feudalism was based on an assemblage of rights and duties so rigidly interdependent that there was no room for a usurper to creep in. The hierarchy of lawful authorities rendered it superfluous to call in extraordinary and extra-legal powers. It is notable, moreover, that Italy, on which Feudalism never established more than a precarious hold, was the first amid the restless, ever-changing life of its cities to restore the figure of a tyrant. We need only call to mind the drama of *Lorenzaccio*.

But now here is a case which merits our careful consideration. Where do we find the first example of the modern dictator? In England. And what is England? The 'Mother of Parliaments'. The country which adopted for itself, and distributed in facsimile throughout the world, the form of parliamentary government. Cromwell makes us wonder whether a dictator is not a necessary concomitant of revolutions, of the rise of democracies and of the establishment of the parliamentary system.

In seventeenth-century England, the Stuarts attempted to play the monarch on the French pattern. But Charles I was not Louis XIII, nor was Buckingham Richelieu. And the English were not the French.

The King and his favourite were by no means devoid of nobility of mind and deportment or of a genuine love of country, but, side by side with these estimable qualities, they exhibited a marked predilection for brilliance and display, together with a great deal of dignity and haughtiness in their bearing and mode of life, all of which things, because a great deal of money was needed to keep them up, grated on the feelings of the English merchants, who by this time had become the wealthiest and most influential element in the country. To this cause of friction between the King and the merchant class, yet another was added: it had to do with religion.

The State religion was the High Church, which was very closely related to Catholicism, and which the city merchants, whose advance in material prosperity was accompanied by an ever increasing desire for wealth and independence, regarded with great hostility because it upheld the principle of authority and practised a costly ceremonial.

That was not the avowed reason of their opposition. The reason alleged was 'Roman corruption' and 'Popery', which the Puritans denounced with veiled faces. Nevertheless, their own corruption was no less reprehensible, the sin of avarice being more heinous than that of prodigality. For that, we have biblical authority, though there is nothing to prevent us from calling on the name of the Lord as we make up the cash.

Oliver Cromwell came of sound country, middle-class stock. This it is important to note, in view of the 'military' side of his career. Born at Huntingdon on the 25th

April, 1599, he followed the calling of a country gentleman, and, if he put himself at the head of a troop of soldiers, it was because nature had endowed him with a genius for command. Had Cromwell been born in the City of London, with the atmosphere of business in his blood and environment, it is most likely that Charles I would never have had his head cut off.

It has been alleged that the Protector as a young man had given himself up to riotous living. Even if it were true, it would be of no great moment. What is much more important to bear in mind is his Welsh and Celtic heredity, which goes far to account for his mysticism, his fanaticism, his love of preaching, his solicitude for the salvation of souls, his feelings, which were moved by passion much rather than by reason. The austere aspect of the country in which his days were passed, accounted for the melancholy, the irritability and the violence which his contemporaries noted in him and to which his deeds sufficiently bear witness.

Oliver Cromwell made his first appearance in public life in the year 1628, as the representative of Cambridge in the House of Commons. That only lasted three months. When Parliament was dissolved, Cromwell went quietly home again.

He settled at St. Ives with his family, and busied himself with cattle-rearing as well as with the organization of Puritan open-air meetings convened for the purpose of counteracting the Catholic influence of the Queen, which was said to be gaining ground at Court, and of stemming the ever-growing power of the High Church which, in the Protestant view, seemed to portend nothing less than the impending submission of England to the Papacy.

In April, 1640, the King found himself in urgent need of money. Parliament, without whose consent he could not obtain it, was therefore again convoked, after an interval of eleven years. Cromwell took his seat for the second time as member for Cambridge.

No sooner had the session begun, than strife broke out between the King and the Commons. The defiant attitude of the latter, and the haughty disdain of the former, rendered agreement impossible. On the 5th May, Charles summoned the Commons to the Bar of the House of Lords and, in angry and contemptuous tones, declared that Parliament was dissolved. Thus ended the Short Parliament, which had sat for just three weeks.

Once again, Oliver returned home. In November, the Houses were again summoned to Westminster and again Cromwell took the road to London. He was now forty years of age, and still quite unknown to fame. One of his fellow-members, Sir Philip Warwick, has sketched his portrait, and it is not a very flattering one. He describes him as 'very ordinarily apparelled' in 'a plain cloth suit, which seemed to have been made by an ill country tailor. His linen was plain, and not very clean; his sword stuck close to his side.' 'His eloquence', adds Sir Philip, 'was full of fervour.' The subject of his speech was hardly reasonable: 'it was a plea for a servant who had dispensed libels against the Queen. I sincerely profess it much lessened my reverence unto that great Council, for he was very much hearkened unto.'

It was not long before matters of graver import, arguments concerning dogma, afforded the member for Cambridge an opportunity to make his mark. In the course of the theological discussions which engaged the attention of the Parliamentary Commissions, Cromwell's mode of speech was dark and apocalyptic, well-calculated to stir the passions of audiences apt to be carried away by religious enthusiasm.

The rift between the King and the Commons continued to widen. The Puritans declared that the King was 'contemptuous', because he refused to argue with men who took their own desires for expressions of the will of God; they said he was 'narrow-minded' because he refused to yield a tittle of the rights of kingship. An understanding between the contending parties was becoming more and more out of the question. The 'Grand Remonstrance', in which all these grievances were assembled, and which was a more emphatic restatement of the 'Petition of Rights', was adopted by Parliament in November, 1640.

Cromwell had largely contributed to bring about this result by the vehemence with which he had supported the measure, telling the members in plain language that when they had the troops at their command, and not before, they would be successful in their conflict with the monarchy. 'Parliament', he said in substance, 'cannot win unless it has an army behind it. You cannot coerce or compel anyone by mere words and phrases. You must have soldiers and weapons.' And it is a fact that, if the English Parliament had not nourished in its bosom a leader capable of raising and commanding an army, and an army able to rout the regular forces of the Crown, it would have met the same fate as that which befel the judicial Parliament of Louis XV, whose members were shown the way home by an escort of dragoons.

At the bottom of Cromwell's power were the Ironsides, just as the blackshirts and the brownshirts are at the back of Mussolini and Hitler. That is a parallel we have met with before. We shall meet with it again.

During the stormy times that marked the winter of 1641, Cromwell began to feel that he was equal to undertaking the leadership of such an army. His instinct was not at fault. It was in war that the real greatness of the man was revealed, and the wonder is that he has not come down to posterity under the title of General Cromwell. It would have given a clearer notion of the nature of his work.

Scarcely was the rupture with the Parliament complete; scarcely had the King left London to put himself at the head of the Royalist troops, when Cromwell threw all his energies into the task of organizing the forces that had decided to throw in their lot with the Parliament.

'I have a lovely company', he wrote to Hampden in September. 'You would respect these soldiers if you knew them.' We cannot help feeling that the man who spoke like that was a born soldier. He loved his men. Like him, they were fired with Puritan zeal, and their dearest aim was to sacrifice their opponents on the altar of their sacred principles. He subjected them to an iron discipline. Having acquitted himself with conspicuous credit in some preliminary skirmishes, he was successively promoted Colonel and Lieutenant-General.

When, at the battle of Marston Moor, which was fought on the 2nd July, 1644, the Puritan army came into conflict with the Royal troops, it was Cromwell and the two thousand five hundred men under his command, who formed its right wing.

The left and the centre were driven in, and Charles's troops were already raising the paean of victory, when Cromwell and his men launched a counter-attack and completely reversed the fortunes of the day. It was from then onward that his men became known as 'Ironsides' and so greatly grew their fame that their very presence on the battlefield was regarded as a sure guarantee of victory for their side.

During a whole year of unbroken successes for the Parliamentary forces, Cromwell's reputation as a military leader continued to increase. Parliament appointed him to the supreme command of the cavalry arm and Cromwell fully justified the confidence thus placed in him, by inflicting a crushing defeat on the Royal troops at Naseby on the 12th June, 1645.

Thus the first Civil War ended in a decisive victory for the Parliamentary forces. They owed their triumph to Cromwell.

For three years, both at Westminster and with the Army, he strove unceasingly to stir up hatred against Charles. It was his constant endeavour to kindle anew the flames of civil war, so that he might get Charles into his power, for he knew well enough that, if Charles eluded him, the Puritan faction would never succeed in imposing their ideas upon the nation. From this, all his subsequent course of action logically proceeded. This was the starting point of a process which finally culminated in the crime of the 9th February, 1649, in the 'cruel necessity' of making away with the King. The deed was as fruitless as it was cruel. The very same day that Charles I was beheaded at Whitehall, Charles II was proclaimed by the Earl of Montrose in Scotland. At the same time, the Catholics of Ireland acknowledged him as their sovereign. Phoenix-like, the Monarchy rose again beneath Cromwell's very eyes. During the King's trial, when Bradshaw, the presiding judge, declared, as he recited the charge, that he spoke 'in the name of the Commons in Parliament assembled, and in that of the good people of England', a voice of angelic sweetness, the voice of Lady Fairfax, was heard to cry, ' 'Tis a lie; not one half, not one quarter of the people of England! Oliver Cromwell is a traitor!' With this, all non-Puritan England heartily concurred. And so it came about that, on the very morrow of the King's death, the country was plunged into direr confusion than ever. Never was the strife of religious sects and civil factions so bitter as in the England of 1650.

No sooner had he gained the upper hand than Cromwell saw almost the whole of England arrayed against him and, had it not been for the disciplined and fanatical army that hedged him round, he would soon have followed Charles to the scaffold. To crown his troubles, dissensions broke out in the very midst of his armed supporters. When the Ironsides marched forth to war, it was, they had been given to understand, to bring about the reign of Liberty, Equality and Fraternity and, more particularly, to secure the equal distribution of wealth. Yet the war, with its harsh discipline and its privations was still going on. And so the Ironsides became the 'Levellers', and claimed the right to help themselves to what they considered their due. Oliver's answer was prompt and inflexible. Just as Robespierre, later on, struck down the *Exagérés*, so Cromwell drowned his 'lovely companies' in blood, and, so doing, regained his dominion over the remainder.

Once more he took his sword in hand to pursue, like the Chosen of the Lord, the fateful path of destiny. Ireland and Scotland revolted 'in the King's name'. Crossing to Ireland, fired with 'bloody wrath', he gained decisive victories at Drogheda and Wexford, and, by the time nine months were over, the rising had been completely repressed. He was now free to deal with Scotland, on whose forces he inflicted crushing defeats at Dunbar and Worcester.

Cromwell has now vanquished all his enemies. He is king in all but name. He takes the name of Lord Protector. All the power is in his hands. What, then, will he do with it? Nothing! Literally nothing! He does not know what form of government to adopt. In his idea, an organization closely resembling the monarchical government would be very expedient, and he proceeds to set up a military régime which seems to the country at large to be a great deal worse than the despotism of Charles I. When his discontented followers said, 'we fought in order that the nation might govern itself according to its choice', Cromwell, in an agony of helplessness replied, 'Yes, but where are we going to find this choice? Among the Episcopalians, the Presbyterians, the Independents, the Anabaptists or the Equalitarians?' In making that reply, Cromwell put his finger on the weak spot in this English experiment in dictatorship.

The adventure was not wanting in irony, but the supreme example of it resides in the fact that the most formidable difficulties the Protector had to cope with had their origin in Parliament.

Cromwell had only taken part in the Civil War in order to force Charles to govern with the consent of Parliament, and now he himself is compelled to admit that he can do nothing at all if he bows to the dictates of that institution. With his customary resolution, regardless of a precedent the memory of which must have been fresh in the minds of all who were present, relying on his troops and still more on his military renown, he marched into Westminster Hall on the 20th April, 1653, and cried in harsh, decisive tones, 'Come, come, we've had enough of this! I'm going to put a stop to this babble of yours,' he went on, while the members sat open-mouthed with astonishment. 'It is not for the profit of these nations, not fit for the common and public good for you to continue here any longer. And therefore I do declare unto you that I do dissolve this Parliament.'

The Members separated without making the smallest show of resistance and, to mark his decision, Cromwell ordered that famous notice of his to be nailed to the door of the Council Chamber, 'Room to Let, unfurnished'.

It was not long, however, before a feeling of loneliness descended upon him. To be quite alone in the midst of a nation rent asunder by disputes which he wearied at last of trying to compose, so oppressed his spirit that as a last resort he made up his mind to summon Parliament yet once again. Fresh disappointments awaited him. Whenever he appealed to the Members to vote some measure designed to bring back order to the distracted country, his majority fell lower and lower and he was more and more bitterly attacked; and, on each occasion, the Protector gained a yet clearer insight into the incompetence, the stubbornness, the futility of the assembly and its proceedings. There's none that bites so fiercely as a wolf turned shepherd. A second session lasted no more than ten days, and on the 4th February, 1658, the members, in formal session assembled, had to listen to these words, 'All this is only playing of the King of Scots his game. The only possible result of it all would be to add to the confusion and bloodshed. I deem it is high time to put an end to your meetings, and I do dissolve this Parliament. Let God judge between you and me.'

That was the last public utterance of Oliver Cromwell. He had come to the end of his strength and of his days. He died on the 3rd September, 1658.

Less than two years later, the people of England went wild with joy as they acclaimed the restoration of Charles II. The only fruit of Cromwell's tremendous effort had been to convince his countrymen that another Stuart was better than a dictator.

Cromwell had gone forth to fight for freedom and the downfall of autocracy. And then, having put himself in power, he had seen that by force, and force alone, was he able to retain and use that power. 'This much being said,' so ran his formula, 'I, or rather the Lord, demand of you . . . " It was a formula that no King, however ardent his belief in the doctrine of Divine Right, would ever have dared to utter, and indeed it would have counted for little if Cromwell had not had his Ironsides at the back of him. The proof is that when the peace-loving Richard Cromwell succeeded his father and proved, almost *ad absurdum*, that he was too courteous to ride rough-shod over such as did not share his views, the whole Cromwellian edifice collapsed like a house of cards and England went back to the Stuarts. Fourteen years of disorder, civil war, slaughter and tyranny had had no definite result save to strengthen the monarchy by making it seem a thing infinitely to be preferred to any substitute.

Since then, the English people have changed dynasties, but they have never again called in an Ironside or a Roundhead to be their ruler.

RICHELIEU

Chronologically speaking, Richelieu should have come before Cromwell; but, in dealing with the famous Cardinal, we find ourselves face to face with an almost unique phenomenon, a phenomenon to which the observers of his own day, with true insight, applied the very appropriate name of *ministériat*, that is to say the well-nigh unfettered control of the State by a prime minister whose acts were invariably ratified by the crown.

It was a form of government which the French people in after years came greatly to admire. At the time, however, the severity of the discipline to which it necessarily gave rise was characterized by those who were compelled to live under it as an abominable tyranny. But to resume.

When on the 14th May, 1610, Ravaillac stabbed Henri IV to the heart, he deemed that he was performing a sacred duty. It was an aftermath of the Wars of Religion. The truth is that Henri's removal from the scene might well have involved the country, then barely recovering from the struggle between the Huguenots and the League, in irretrievable disaster.

The immense work of consolidation to which the great ruler had set his hand was then but hardly begun and if that patchwork expedient, the Edict of Nantes, had dispelled the Protestant menace for the time being, the great feudal leaders were only awaiting a favourable opportunity in order to recover from the King of France all those powers and prerogatives of which the successor of Hugh Capet had deprived them for the benefit of the Crown.

Sully has recorded that, on the morrow of the murder in the Rue de la Ferronnerie, people were saying in the lobbies of the Louvre, 'Kings have had their day. The Princes and the great nobles are coming into their own.' The idea was by no means an extravagant one.

What obstacles to the fulfilment of their ambitions were firebrands like Condé, Vendôme, Bouillon, Nevers, Mayenne and Soissons likely to encounter? The Queen Regent, a woman of no very marked intelligence, the King, a stripling of just over eighteen summers, a group of elderly ministers derisively nicknamed 'The Dodderers', in short, a feeble government whom, by fair means or foul, they counted on bending to their will.

They came within a hair's breadth of success, and the Kingdom narrowly escaped being laid waste by a fresh outbreak of the civil strife which had so grievously afflicted it throughout the previous century. Happily, the nobles failed to agree among themselves.

To the turbulence of the great nobles was added the twofold menace of a recrudescence of religious dissension, and the inordinate ambition of the House of Austria. Threatened with peril within and peril without, one thing and one thing only, could preserve the unity of the French nation, and that was the iron hand. And at this juncture, the good genius of France did indeed so order it that Louis XIII should realize that he, unaided, was unequal to the task before him, and that, setting aside his personal likes and dislikes, he should betake himself to a man whom, indeed, he little loved, but whose energy he had judged at its true worth, to wit, Cardinal de Richelieu.

Richelieu's government was in very truth a dictatorship. What was so original — and so effective — about his handling of the situation was that he relied almost wholly on the monarchical and national principle, as we interpret it to-day, and that he made everything subservient to the power and prestige of the King, as being the incarnate symbol of the nation. All the Cardinal's actions were subordinated to this transcending motive.

Playwrights and novelists have freely distorted the figures of Louis XIII and his minister, representing the one as a cunning and timorous weakling, the other as a man possessed with a mania for despotic cruelty.

All this is very far removed from the truth. It must be allowed that Louis XIII proved himself a far less brilliant monarch than either his father or his son; but he also proved that he possessed undeniable insight and understanding by giving ungrudging support to the minister who served him so well, and by standing between him and an opposition who succeeded in enlisting, against the task he had undertaken, the two queens, the royal princes, the nobility and a good half of the country.

That task Richelieu had defined as soon as he came into power and it is set out in his *Political Testament*: 'When Your Majesty decided to admit me to your counsels and to accord me a large measure of your confidence, I promised to employ all my industry and all the authority with which it pleased you to invest me, to break up the Huguenot party, to humble the pride of the great nobles and to restore your name to the position it was entitled to occupy among the rulers of foreign countries.'

The first two points were necessarily antecedent to the third, and there is no doubt that they gave the minister infinitely more anxiety.

As soon as he took his seat on the Council, the Cardinal's position became a predominant one. Since his rapid rise to power — it had taken him four months, from November 1616 to April 1617, to achieve it — six years ago, he had devoted himself to a careful study of the problems of the diplomatic situation and considered how best to accomplish the reforms on which his heart was set. From the very outset, at the very earliest meetings in which he took a part, he gave his interlocutors, and particularly Louis XIII, a wonderful impression of clear-headedness, energy and strength of will, which the latter, up to then, had found in no other of his advisers. It retained his confidence for a long time to come.

Richelieu had need of that confidence for, from the very beginning, he had to contend with the blind, tenacious and fierce opposition of all who thought their privileges in peril, or apprehended some interference with their schemes for self-aggrandizement. At this period, the notion of patriotism was not what it is to-day. Great personages in the State had no compunction about entering into negotiations with foreign princes with a view to resisting this or that government plan when they considered it detrimental to their interests.

It was against these that Richelieu directed his earliest efforts.

Kept duly apprised of what was afoot by the remarkable intelligence service which he had organized in France and abroad, the Cardinal never hesitated to make an example of the culprit, no matter what his rank, for he had made it clear to the King that leniency would completely nullify the measures he had introduced with the object of strengthening the royal authority and increasing the country's prestige.

He was no less ruthless with the instigators of civil war, but, if he punished with a heavy hand, it was to make men understand that a change had taken place in France, and that high lineage was no longer a guarantee that dangerous games could be played with the impunity his predecessors had hitherto accorded them.

It is necessary to bear this in mind if we wish to appreciate the underlying motives of his domestic policy and to justify the means he adopted to secure its success.

His most famous 'victims', Chalais, Montmorency, Cinq-Mars, de Thou, were just ordinary traitors. Because intrepid amazons and lovely dames were involved in their intrigues, they have long been enveloped in a perfumed aureole of adventure and romance. The plain truth is they were mere political criminals.

The principal, and almost sole, object of the successive execution of these men was to make it clear to the great ones of the land who had been stirring up trouble ever since the death of Henri IV, that the time had come to obey, and that if they did not, their heads would be in jeopardy.

In consequence, Richelieu incurred their mortal hatred and they vowed that he should die. Ten times their plots came within an ace of success.

It was only by a series of miracles that the Cardinal escaped assassination. But it argued a very imperfect knowledge of the man to suppose that it was possible to subdue his courage. Relying with confidence on the support of his royal master, he never relaxed his severity in any matters that threatened to compromise the sovereignty of his lord the King, or the safety of the Realm.

Until his dying day, he was forced to go on fighting; but the last word was with him, and the head of Cinq-Mars was, if one may so express it, the winning trick in the long contest between the great nobles and the Crown, a contest in which the former were vanquished without any hope of raising their heads again for many a day to come.

Even in these days a descendant of one of these noble families will often be heard to say, 'My family had two châteaux; one was destroyed by Richelieu, the other by the Revolutionaries'.

Side by side with the work of bringing the greater nobles to heel, Richelieu continued to pursue the task of crushing the Huguenots, who aimed at nothing short of the disruption of the kingdom. The whole work of monarchical consolidation and national expansion, to which the Bishop of Luçon had set his hand, was threatened with destruction by the growth of the Protestant faction who, under the cloak of a fervent solicitude for virtue and morality, aimed at overthrowing the old Catholic and Roman order, and setting up in its place individualistic institutions of anti-monarchical tendencies.

Richelieu could not endure them; chiefly because his whole policy was directed towards buttressing the throne, but also because peace at home was essential to the success of the far-reaching measures on which he proposed to embark. What, moreover, was the good of humbling the nobles, if a whole section of the population could entrench themselves behind the ramparts of fortified towns and snap their fingers at the edicts and the soldiers of the King? All that had been done, and all that remained to do, might be gravely compromised if the Huguenot leaders threw open the seaports and other places of access, to the warships and mercenaries of their English allies.

Wholly preoccupied with a formidable duel with a foreign power which tested his skill and strength to the utmost, it was impossible for Richelieu to go on being haunted with the idea that the foe might be helped to get a footing on French soil by Frenchmen, and be maintained by them. What alternative, then, had he but to crush the insurgents before their rebellion had a chance to succeed.

In order to be beforehand with them he brought all the resources of his genius into play, taking upon himself a task of incredible magnitude and complexity. Like Mussolini to-day, he assumed the personal control of the chief offices of State. To the direction of Home and

Foreign Affairs he added the War Office, the Treasury, the Admiralty and the duties of Commander-in-Chief.

He was to be seen at la Rochelle in jack-boots and breastplate, his sword girt on, serving the guns, taking charge of the siege-works, and superintending the construction of the famous boom. His health was indifferent, his life in constant peril, but still his courage was undaunted. His indomitable will battered a way, through every obstacle, to victory.

The fall of la Rochelle meant checkmate to the Protestants. They had been guilty of a twofold crime. Not content with using their artillery against the soldiers of the King, they had called in the foreigner to help them. Their one hope now lay in the clemency of the victor. It is true that in their first interview with the Cardinal they endeavoured to make conditions, but they soon lowered their tone. Their lives were spared.

But the insurrection was not yet over. Repressed at la Rochelle, it reared its head again in the South. Richelieu, who was in Italy campaigning with the King, hurriedly despatched his royal master to suppress this latest outbreak. The measures taken to effect this object were stern to the point of cruelty, for the situation permitted of no delay. On the 28th June, 1629, the Duc de Rohan, for the Protestants, and Richelieu for the King, put their signatures to the Treaty of Alès, thus completing the discomfiture of the former.

Victorious all along the line, the Cardinal was farseeing and astute enough not to press his triumph unduly. He even prevailed on Louis XIII to mitigate the severity of the conditions at first proposed. For Richelieu was

more anxious to rally his late adversaries to support the
Crown by laying the foundations of a lasting and equitable peace, than to sow the seeds of a smouldering and
incurable resentment. He therefore contented himself
with depriving them of their fortified places, which was
equivalent to disarming them. They were to be free to
practise their religion without molestation, and the
King pledged himself to make no distinction between
his subjects.

This really amounted to a reversion to the terms laid
down by the Edict of Nantes. Ruthless and inexorable
as had been his conduct of the war, hostilities were no
sooner at an end, than Richelieu—guided by policy rather
than inclination — displayed a notable spirit of forbear-
ance and conciliation.

It had taken him two years and six months to pacify
the Kingdom. Such a signal success naturally cemented
still more firmly the confidence which the King reposed
in his Minister, with the result that the understanding
between them bore fruit in an ever closer collaboration.
Not that the King trusted blindly to his minister. As
we have recently learnt from the valuable researches of
M. Louis Battifol, the King often acted on his own
initiative, nor did the two men always see eye to eye.
But the King never turned a wilfully deaf ear to his
minister's arguments, and never failed to support him,
as witness the famous 'Day of Dupes' when Richelieu,
proving himself too strong for the King's own mother,
forced her to tread the path of exile.

Richelieu had now rid himself of the Protestant in-
cubus and, for the time being, the conspirators, whose

avowed object it was to expedite his passage to another world, suspended their activities. He was therefore free to turn his attention to the third item in his programme, the humiliation of the House of Austria.

That aim he pursued with the passionate ardour he always displayed whenever the greatness of his country was involved For ten long years he had, by subtle manœuvring, successfully kept his country out of war. But now the time had come when a further postponement of the conflict was impossible. At first, the fortunes of war were against him, but soon, thanks to his accurate appreciation of the elements necessary to ensure success, victory crowned his efforts. Though he had again to defend himself against another of those conspiracies at home which had used up half his life, he bore with him to the grave the certainty that his work would live behind him.

In eighteen years of dictatorship, based on the royal sanction, Richelieu had laid the foundations of the modern state. He knew that all had not been done, that all could not have been done, yet, with his insight into the nature of things, he was able to assure himself, in the light of the ground already covered, that he was opening a path of unlimited possibilities to those who would be called upon to succeed him. Well chosen and obedient coadjutors, a nobility taught its place, a noble and enduring example, old usages restored, a common spirit animating the whole community from the top of the ladder to the bottom, and finally, a civil service willing and able to serve the public with conscientious-ness, all these things contributed to facilitate that efflorescence of national greatness and glory for the sake of which he had sacrificed every moment of his life. Such, as we of this later day have come to recognize, were the fruits of Richelieu's ministerial dictatorship.

And what came after him? Again a King in his minority and a woman-regent. An attempt was made to carry on the system of the French Cardinal by entrusting the direction of affairs to a Cardinal of Italian origin, for the sole and simple reason that he was on the spot and was the most intelligent of the four advisers appointed by Louis XIII. Anne of Austria had recourse to a remarkable expedient to ensure that Mazarin should continue in her service. She secretly married him. The fact now seems beyond dispute. It need not cause us over-much astonishment, for Mazarin, though he wore the Roman purple, had never taken orders.

A foreigner, lacking alike the dignity and the prestige of Richelieu, Mazarin was even less to the public taste than his predecessor had been, and he became frankly unpopular. All those whom the great Cardinal had sent about their business, now sought their revenge. That aim expressed itself in the Fronde, a seventeenth-century essay in experimental revolution; but the political weapon which Richelieu had left behind him enabled the astute Mazarin to triumph over his adversaries. Nevertheless, the verdict had gone forth. The French people had had enough of *ministériats*. But as the country had nearly relapsed into Anarchy again, through the Frondist revolt, only one resource remained to it, the direct rule of the King; in other words, monarchical autocracy.

That is why Louis XIV's first pronouncement on attaining his majority was the famous apophthegm 'L'Etat, c'est moi!' All France applauded that utterance. And indeed the observation was interpreted as announcing, not a despotism, but a deliverance. Henceforth the State was, not a minister, nor the great nobles and fair ladies of the Fronde, nor the magistrates of Parliament, nor the lords of Finance (hence the importance and the significance of the Fouquet trial). The governing power would now be in the undisputed possession of its lawful representative, the heir to the Kings of France.

LOUIS XIV: DICTATOR AND KING

IT will then not be a matter for astonishment if we include the great King in the ranks of the dictators, although the idea of dictatorship is generally held to signify the substitution of a temporary, for a normal and regular form of government. But such a view of the matter has in reality no *a priori* validity, inasmuch as the proper aim of a dictator being to restore, or to establish, a stable government for the benefit of the State, it was precisely with that aim that Louis XIV was constantly occupied.

As heir apparent, Louis XIV was naturally called on to succeed his father, but from his earliest days, saddened as he had been, and humiliated, by the Fronde, he made up his mind to be a King indeed, to impress his will upon his subjects to whatever order they belonged, no matter how exalted their birth, no matter how distinguished their services to the State. No other sovereign of the Capet dynasty had ever set his heart so ardently on personal ascendancy, none had ever been so ready to assume the responsibilities of government.

Doubtless we must beware of conjuring up an *a posteriori* picture of a youthful prince uniting in his person all the virtues of an experienced statesman with the seductive charm of youth. Before attaining the wisdom which we find so striking and so moving in the Memoirs which he began to write at the age of thirty, the son of Louis XIII had served his apprenticeship both as a man and a monarch. But one of his earliest and clearest ideas, one that was pregnant with the happiest consequences, was that it was his duty, at all costs, to preserve the throne and the nation from the perils of any renewal of civil conflict.

The memory of the Fronde abode with him all his days, and it was on that account that he established himself at Versailles, away from Paris and its revolutions. The bitter recollections he retained of the Frondist rebellion were fixed in his mind by Mazarin's commentaries which, demonstrating the relationship of cause and effect, proved to him how necessary it was that France should have a stable government. Louis, whose temper was by nature autocratic, took the lesson to heart and never forgot it. If he exalted the throne to the height he did, it was in order to put it beyond the reach of injury, or even the threat of injury, investing it with such power and splendour as to deter each and all, no matter whom, from even dreaming of raising a hand against it.

Therefore the King determined, as soon as death had freed him from Mazarin's control, to make it clear that he intended to govern alone, to give his orders direct, and, if necessary, to enforce their observance. Hardly had the Cardinal given up the ghost, than Louis summoned a meeting of his ministers and forbade them to take any action without his consent. Next day, the Archbishop of Rouen, president of the Clerical Assembly, put the following question to him. 'Your Majesty' he said, 'ordered me to refer all matters to M. le Cardinal. But the Cardinal is dead. To whom, then, does Your Majesty now wish me to refer them?' 'To me, my lord Archbishop,' answered the twenty-three-year-old King.

So out of harmony were these resolutions with the traditions and ideas then current, that the whole thing seemed to the Court like a miniature *coup d'état*. They would not believe their ears, and report has it that, when Anne of Austria was informed of what her son had said, she burst into a fit of laughter.

But they did not reckon with the King's will. Deeming that to play the part of absolute monarch effectively he would need to know the ins and outs of State business, he set to work in earnest. Every day, for hours on end, he conferred with his Secretaries of State, perused and annotated their reports, drew up lists of questions, to which the ministers were required to give clear, concise answers.

Endowed with a splendid constitution, Louis XIV was able to give full play to a young man's taste for pleasure, without the slightest prejudice to the punctual observance of his royal duties — his *metiér de roi* as he expressed it. Thus he began an undeviating ascent to greatness towards which he strove with that unceasing application which Charles Maurras has well described as a glowing fire of resolution and reason — *une ardeur de volonté et de raison*.

The French people were quick to realize the deep significance of the King's ideas, or rather, perhaps, it was the King who grasped what it was that France required. France gave him a free hand and thus enabled him to abolish the final vestiges of ancient wrongs, and to display to the world the inspiring picture of a prince and his people working harmoniously to a common end, for the like of which we should search through history in vain.

We know what came of it — the '*pré carré*' all but completed; in Europe, the prestige of France raised to a
height that has never been surpassed; amazing prosperity
at home; literature and the arts flourishing as never
before; our frontiers inviolate for a century — in a word
the Age of Louis XIV!

The King's whole heart, it must be borne in mind,
was in his work. The zeal with which he had from the
beginning begun to tutor and instruct himself, never
flagged. For fifty-four years he applied himself day by
day to affairs of State, discussing, considering, weighing
and deciding, with that wonderful clearheadedness which
so amazed Sainte-Beuve. No step of any importance, at
home or abroad, was ever decided upon without the
King having played his part in the deliberations. Never,
not even in the days when his most famous ministers,
such as Colbert or Louvois or Lionne, were rendering
him such brilliant service, did he allow them entire
freedom of action. There was to be no reviving that
'*ministériat*' of which the French people had grown so
heartily sick. Until his dying day, he always let them
know that he was King, as he had said he would when
he was a young man of twenty.

It has been said, and the saying has been repeated in
season and out, that, just before he died, he blamed
himself for having been too much given to waging war.
But when people are inclined triumphantly to urge this
point against Louis XIV, we have asked them whether
they would be willing to give up Lille, Strasbourg and
Besançon, and we have never succeeded in getting an
answer.

Now for an outline of what followed.

Louis XV, who is better known to-day, and more fairly dealt with by his later biographers (see, in particular, M. Pierre Gaxotte's book) Louis XV did his best — it is Voltaire's opinion — to carry on the régime of Louis XIV in thought and action. Where he failed was not in brains, but in character. He saw what ought to be done clearly enough, but he had not the necessary strength of will to see that it was carried out. However, he dealt faithfuly with the refractory Parliaments. He refused to convoke the States-General because, he said prophetically, it would spell the ruin of the Kingdom. His saying, 'After me, the deluge', is a typical example of how proverbs come to be misunderstood. Louis XV did not mean to say that he did not care what happened after him. But he had a presentiment that, when he died, the heavens would open.

The prophecy was fulfilled by Louis XVI, who gave a free rein to everyone and everything that had been curbed and repressed since Louis XIV's accession; that is to say for rather more than a hundred years. He wanted to play the part of a royal reformer. It did not occur to him that, in order to take the lead in a scheme of reform, one must make sure of one's own position first. If he had had a more thorough knowledge of his times, he would have seen that the eighteenth century, though it loved light, did not hate despotism. He took his cue from the popularity which a ruler a hundred times more autocratic than he enjoyed in France, from his own brother-in-law Joseph, or it may be from Frederick of Prussia.

THE VOGUE OF THE
ENLIGHTENED DESPOT

THE notion of dictatorship in the eighteenth century had of necessity to undergo some important modifications brought about, not only by new ideas, but, at least as much, by the living examples, which exert a different sort of influence.

Daring as were its ideas in regard to religious and social matters, in politics, contrary to what is generally supposed, it nearly always respected the established order of things, so far at least as general principles were concerned. Criticism was almost wholly confined to details — though these details, it must be confessed, were by no means unimportant. But it must not for a moment be imagined that the kingly office, for example, was the object of attack. Although the Encyclopaedists did not invariably give utterance to all they thought in their inmost hearts, and although on several points they were impelled to maintain a certain reserve, there are strong grounds for thinking that there were very few Republicans amongst them.

Even about Diderot there is no small measure of doubt. As for Voltaire, it is beyond question that he had a preference for personal government. He did not assume the role of apologist for the age of Louis XIV and Louis XV for nothing. Jean Jacques Rousseau himself, the author of the *Contrat Social*, who, incidentally, was quite opposed to Voltaire in views and temperament, considerably toned down his Genevan doctrines when it was no longer a question of legislating *in vacuo*, but of giving practical advice to nations who came to ask him to frame a constitution for them, such as the Corsicans, or the Poles. Moreover, deeply imbued though he was with respect for the republican form of government, he held the view that it was only suited to little countries, and pronounced emphatically against it for a big nation like France. Furthermore, we shall find, in the *Contrat Social* itself, an apology for dictators.

At bottom, the eighteenth-century philosophers were, above all, for progress, for enlightenment, which had to be forcibly imposed on the crowd of imbeciles that would insist on clinging to their old prejudices, especially their religious ones. England was admired, but without much sincerity. There has always been a certain amount of Anglo-mania in France. A little later, Franklin and the American democracy excited a great deal of enthusiasm, on the principle of 'whatever's new is always good', and because these things were happening in a new country a long way off. In their hearts and minds, the reformers, taken on the whole, were much more impressed by the European model known as 'the Enlightened Dictator'.

The eighteenth century had, indeed, witnessed the emergence of a very special form of monarchy which, as in the person of Louis XIV, may be looked upon as uniting in one and the same person, the pomp and power of a king, with the pomp and power of a dictator. And even with the philosophers, who hold the monarchs of Central or Eastern Europe in admiration, it is very certain that the prestige of the dictators eclipsed the prestige of the kings.

For tradition had but little weight with them. By the historical and hereditary aspects of monarchy they set small store. The essential element resided in the continuity of policy adopted by a man of force and character who, with the laws of sound reason to back him, imposed his will on all alike. Thus to the chances of an election, the philosophers were led to prefer another sort of chance, that of birth, which has little to do with monarchy proper and which from time to time sets on the throne a friend of progress and enlightenment. This it is that, later on, Renan came to describe as 'benevolent despotism'.

Naturally, mere theory carried less weight than concrete examples — though the examples, it may be, were not always understood. For it certainly appears that in the undisputed collaboration of the Kings and the Philosophers, the Kings were the predominant partners and that they got a great deal more out of the philosophers than the philosophers got out of them. But at any rate, Frederick II of Prussia, Catherine the Great, and Joseph II, Marie Therése's successor to the various thrones of Bohemia and Hungary and to the still venerable title of the old Holy German Empire, were, for many long years, sacred *simulacra*, so to speak, of the Dictator-King, to which the philosophers addressed their reasoned, and sometimes rationalistic, petitions.

It is difficult to arrive at an exact idea of what an enlightened despot really was, for the theory of this very exceptional type of government had never been clearly defined. First and foremost, the enlightened despot, duly guided by the laws of natural philosophy, had to be an adversary of the Church. On this point, the philosophers got plenary satisfaction. Frederick II was a Lutheran. Catherine II was Empress of an orthodox country in which religion had, indeed, a deep and widespread influence, but in which, on account of the ignorance of the clergy, it was easy to say to it, 'Thus far and no farther!' As for the Hapsburg-Lorraine family, it is true that Marie-Thérèse, who shed tears over the partition of Poland, though she did not refuse her share of it, was a great deal too devout. For this reason her son Joseph II was regarded as greatly to be preferred, for even during her reign, and chiefly during her quarrels with the papacy, he proved himself the very type and exemplar of the anti-clerical sovereign.

This was the only point on which the philosophers really insisted. It may perhaps have escaped them that, in reality, this anti-clericalism only added to their despot's might. But what cared they for that, if only they could get the Jesuits bundled out of Portugal and elsewhere, and, — a notable triumph for the free-thinkers this! — persuade the Pope himself to dissolve their order?

However, illumined by Reason's radiant beam, these rulers gave other causes for satisfaction. Catherine sent for Diderot to come to Russia, and asked his advice about educating the Moujiks. The advice, however, remained a dead letter and the majority of the social-reform schemes on which the enlightened despots of the eighteenth century had set their hearts seem to have been chiefly destined to enhance their reputation with friends who were by no means exacting in their demands, and who undertook to see that they were well advertised.

That which constitutes the real character of an aristocratic ruler like Catherine of Russia, of an absolute monarch like Frederick, viz: their almost unvarying cynicism, their boundless admiration of force and intelligence, was no doubt well enough understood by an epoch which had produced these astonishing exemplars of political humanity. But not much was said about them. No attempt was made to understand how it was that, following in the steps of Ivan and Peter, Catherine's place was pre-eminently in the ranks of the champions of Russian territorial aggrandizement, nor did it dawn on people in general that her philosophizing was mere camouflage. It never occurred to them that Frederick II was much more of an Empire-builder than a royal philosopher. Perhaps the only people in France to see it were Louis XV and his ministers who, contrary to the trend of public opinion, and sensing peril in Prussia's rising star, sought to counteract it by an Austrian alliance.

The foreign rulers that were held up to popular admiration were commended for having so admirably understood — as dictators always should — the value of certain acts and certain shibboleths. Just as to-day one has to talk of modern myths and to indulge in the usual party oratory, so in those days it was the thing to prate a lot about Reason, to denounce the tyranny of the Church, to tear people away from their ancient beliefs. Sacrifice, too, had to be paid to some abstract idea of 'man' whereof the American Declaration of Rights, preceding the French, drew an unrecognizable portrait. When Joseph II stamped out the risings in the Low Countries and essayed to reduce his vast and ramshackle Empire to a unity that, perhaps, did violence to nature, he was sacrificing to this idol.

But at the same time, Emperor, Empress, King, lauded to the skies by the publicists of France, augment their power, and increase, or at least dream of increasing, the stability of their thrones. That is a fact that should make us reflect. While the philosophers were acclaiming the princes who subscribed to the Encyclopaedia and made Voltaire, d'Alembert or Diderot welcome at their courts, these same princes were placing their reliance on force, on the ideas of the day, and did not disdain for that purpose the additional power with which tradition invested them. Joseph II did not repudiate the doctrine of Divine Right, and Catherine invariably required to be obeyed by the Sacred Synod, to which she always sent her representative.

Far, then, from being a more liberal form of government, the 'enlightened despotism' of the eighteenth century seems to have been a particularly interesting species of dictatorship, for it mingled all the old reasons which the few can have for dominating the many, with other ideas of more recent date, which may indeed be merely pretexts but which are of singular service to the manifold designs of despots. We see them being crowned by their Churches, saluting the priests of the new spirit even as Constantine, when Pontifex Maximus, saluted the Christian bishops, while a few traces of seeming demagogy only serve to enhance their power and to give greater impetus to their propaganda.

It is none the less true that the idea of 'Enlightened despotism', temporarily obscured in France by the Revolution, was destined to regain its full force with Napoleon Bonaparte, and to contribute in considerable measure to the establishment of the Consulate and the Empire. It is absolutely impossible, if, duly respecting historical sequence, we would arrive at a correct understanding of our own era, to ignore the idea entertained by intellectual aristocrats, that progress cannot proceed from the credulous, plodding and stupid multitude, but that it must be imposed from above by supermen.

ROBESPIERRE

WHEN the Revolution of 1789 broke out, no one suspected that it was the herald of the Republic. According to Aulard, the historian, there were not then ten republicans in the whole of France. Nor, when the Republic was proclaimed, did anyone suppose that it was going to culminate in a dictatorship. Still less were the French aware that, in shouting for Liberty, the thing that they really wanted was Equality, that Equality is the sworn foe of Liberty, that one must be sacrificed to the other, and that, in consequence, it needs a strong government to break down social inequalities. Little though they realized it, the French people were aiming at an autocracy.

The Republic 'one and indivisible' had at last been proclaimed. The power of the State was concentrated, not so much in the Convention, but, to a much greater extent, in two Committees. One, the Committee of General Surety, whose activities remained latent and obscure until the crisis of the 9th Thermidor, which it had provoked. The other, the Committee of Public Safety. In this latter, three personages lorded it over the rest. They were a young man of twenty-six named Saint-Just, handsome, vainglorious, but a marvellous orator; Couthon a cripple, who had to be wheeled about in an invalid chair, cruel as Marat and sometimes as keen-sighted, and, lastly — Robespierre!

Robespierre was the fine flower of the Revolution,

Robespierre in those few months of his ascendancy, months which soon began to seem like years. For the rest, Mirabeau, Danton — they did but pass across the stage. They never had all the power to themselves. Moreover they were discredited by the scandal of their private lives, especially their monetary transactions, which were notorious. It is impossible, in these days, to hold a brief for Danton; and the India Company scandal, which involved his tools and his friends in irretrievable ruin, remains a lasting blot upon his memory. No scandal of any sort ever tarnished the personal fame of Robespierre. That is why the others, who were themselves corrupt, called him the Incorruptible.

When the Revolution began, Maximilien de Robespierre was thirty-one years of age, having been born at Arras on the 6th May, 1758. He attended college there, attracting the favourable notice of the Bishop, and then proceeded to complete his studies at the Lycée Louis le Grand in Paris. In 1781, having obtained his degree and qualified as a barrister, he returned to Arras, where he lived a quiet, orderly life, inditing amatory verses, and occasionally appearing on behalf of a client at the Law Courts. Apparently no existence could have been more unexciting. Finding himself, in no long time, a member of the Arras Academy, he became familiar with what was a usual subject of discussion at provincial academies in those days, namely the philosophy of revolution. In 1789, he was elected to the 'Constituante' and, like everybody else, he was a royalist.

However, Rousseau's teaching had a profound effect on him, and little by little, he came to grasp the trend of the events that were taking place about him. After the flight to Varennes, he clamoured for the dethronement of the King. Under the Legislative Assembly he became a Republican. The Convention saw him a Montagnard. Thus, with sure and unfaltering steps, he kept pace with the Revolution, never lagging behind it, never outstripping it. On the 16th April, 1790, he became president of the Jacobin Club. To the very end, he remained a model Jacobin. What makes it so hard to understand the man is, first and foremost, that he seems so little human. For a long time, he was no small enigma to the more ardent apologists of the Revolution. Danton, for all his vices and passions, was a thing of flesh and blood. Robespierre was incorruptible, no doubt. But his was the incorruptibility of a mineral, of a diamond. The laws of ordinary humanity did not seem to apply to him. He was the Jacobin Club's conception of a man, as Michelet was the first to observe. He was a walking abstraction. He thought of nothing, cared for nothing, outside the Revolution. To that he was devoted, body and soul. After all, he died for it. He was a revolutionary, yet he was able to play the conservative at need, and he was pure, yet his purity did not prevent him from yielding, contemptuously, in cases where compromise was inevitable. He was the priest of an unknown god, a god who would sometimes seem to have revealed himself to him alone.

'Unknown' is an apt description, for the conception of the Revolution to which Robespierre bowed the knee was by no means easy to understand. Like the rest of them Robespierre had sung the hymn of Progress, set

Reason on a pedestal and attacked the Church. However, when the Hebertist campaign developed, when it was found that the priests who had taken the oath were no better off than those who had not, Robespierre put the brake on the movement. Though a disciple of Rousseau and an admirer of the Vicaire Savoyard, he was undoubtedly sincere. If there was anything he realized with especial clearness, it was the importance to the State of an established religion, as fostering a race of well-behaved and law-abiding citizens. The India Company scandal, which broke out at this juncture and showed up the extent to which parliamentary corruption had gained ground, afforded him an opportunity of dealing a simultaneous blow at the 'Indulgents' and the 'Enragés', Danton and Hébert. Immediately afterwards, Robespierre delivered a speech on the relation between moral ideas and republican convictions. Without further ado, the Convention recognized the existence of the Supreme Being and a great festival was held in honour of the Father of the Universe. This marked the zenith of Robespierre's career. Here we put our finger on the complexity of his religious and political ideas. We must not forget that this man, who was the Protagonist of the Terror, was nevertheless supported by the Assembly's Right, and (though secretly) by the Catholics. For the feeling had somehow got abroad that it was Robespierre who was the man destined to bring back social order. If he had lived, the Concordat would have been signed by him and not by Bonaparte.

And so it was for the rest. A strong Communist movement was represented in the Assembly by Jacques Roux.

After Jacques Roux had disappeared, Hébert and Chaumette, afraid of being side-tracked, took up his programme and fiercely attacked the Convention, accusing it of starving the people and of shielding the speculators in public funds. In the Committee of Public Safety, two followers of Hébert, Collot d'Herbois and Billaud-Varennes, soon joined the ranks of the extremists. Partial bankruptcy, taxation of wheat, legislation regarding 'cornering', price-regulation, mass-levies, commandeering of labour, such were the principal measures associated with the social and economic Revolution.

All these measures, inspired and promoted by the whole-hoggers, Robespierre accepted and adopted as his own, though sometimes not without reluctance, it would seem. If he had not been overthrown, what would he have done? This is a branch of the game of hypothetical history to which someone has given the name of *Ouchrony*. There is ground for thinking that, while retaining the essential features of Hébert's and Roux's programme, Robespierre would have agreed to a certain amount of give and take, and have adopted a less uncompromising attitude, just as Lenin, after a spell of undiluted communism, inaugurated the N.E.P.

He was handicapped by his incorruptibility, by his want of tact and by the general apathy. He seemed to be bent on justifying the exaggerations of the propagandists, who represented him as a tiger athirst for blood. The Great Terror, which day by day sent whole batches of innocent people to the guillotine, had turned the stomachs of the Parisian populace. Robespierre never realized this and sincerely intended

97

to stop the Terror when the Revolution had been purged of its impurities.

On the 26th July he delivered a speech before the Convention which had a considerable effect upon his audience. He spoke of purging the Committee of General Surety, the Committee of Public Safety and the Assembly. He demanded the creation of a new financial system, and launched a vigorous attack upon Billaud-Varennes and the Communist measures. All those who were the objects of his threats were filled with terror. They secretly disseminated the report that he was aiming at absolute control of the State. On the ground that at the Festival of the Supreme Being he had marched at the head of the Convention, they accused him of reviving the processional pageantry of royalty.

The Committee of General Surety, which, since the affair of the India Company, had been somewhat in the shade, led the campaign. Fouché and Tallien negotiated with the Plain. On the 27th July, the 9th Thermidor according to the Revolutionary calendar, Robespierre was found guilty of playing the dictator, and was guillotined the next day.

With him ended the first attempt at revolutionary dictatorship that France had yet experienced. Abroad, no one had been taken in. Men talked of 'Robespierre's fleet', of 'Robespierre's army'. He was looked upon as the revolutionary incarnation of his country, the born ring-leader of riot and disorder.

And such indeed he was. But his case is significant, because in him we behold a man completely identified with the Revolution and yet compelled by the invincible nature of things to accommodate himself to facts. So it is that he offers the somewhat unusual example of an abstract theorist running in double harness with a practical statesman. Had it not been for Robespierre, it is very probable that Napoleon Bonaparte would never have been possible.

NAPOLEON BONAPARTE

AFTER the fall of Robespierre, the most urgent task for those who had overthrown him was to make short work of both the Republic and the Dictatorship. There was no question of going back to the unworkable Constitution of 1793, which was never put into operation, and which was vainly and everlastingly lamented by all true Republicans. The need of the hour was a strong and stable government and, most important of all, one which would be able to keep clear of bankruptcy. On the other hand, no one wanted a return of a bloodthirsty tyranny like Robespierre's. For some little time, a Triumvirate was on the *tapis*. Men who had been brought up on Latin history liked the sound of the word. Yet everyone knew that there is always a Caesar, or an Octavius, who gets rid of the other two. And 'the high-handed men' on the Committee of Public Safety, Couthon, Saint-Just and Robespierre were surely a case in point. A very deceptive triumvirate, theirs! It had soon resolved itself into a government of one, a monarchy in other words. So the triumvirate idea was discarded in favour of a Directory of Five. This was adulterating the 'pure Republic' with a vengeance. But who cared a fig for the 'pure Republic' now? Why, Sieyès who, years ago, had been so anxious to raise up the Third Estate from nothing to something, even he did not feel easy in his mind about it, and virtually plotted its overthrow. He was the first of the Brumaire conspirators. The problem was this:

Men had to choose between the Republic and the Revolution. All those who were mixed up with the Revolution, and chiefly the regicides, would throw over the Republic without a qualm. And in no long time, Republic and Directory alike, sapped by war abroad and dissentions at home, by bankruptcy and by scandals, were shorn of every democratic virtue. The triumvirate had been shelved, but it was coming back again. We know how, and through whom. The fateful day, the day which good Republicans like Michelet and Hugo so long regarded as the day when the great crime was finally consummated, was the 18th Brumaire!

The 18th Brumaire at last brought to the front of the stage the most celebrated dictator of modern times. Stolid, hard-headed men still glow with pride when they think of his story. Neither Pericles nor Caesar fires the leaders of our day with such enthusiasm. Mussolini, for example, takes him for his model. His name is Napoleon Bonaparte.

If we want to amuse ourselves with speculating on 'the might have been', there is no better subject than he. 'What would have happened if . . .?' What would have happened, if Louis XV had not annexed Corsica to· France in 1768, to the parents, poor but proud, of that child (their fourth) who was destined to be the founder of a dynasty? What would have happened if Charles Bonaparte had not died three years before the Revolution? He would have become a deputy of the *noblesse*, possibly a liberal. Most likely he would have been guillotined, or forced to emigrate, and his son, held back by the paternal precept and the paternal example, would not have felt quite so free with regard to certain coming events. Your dictator must nearly always have an accomplice — and the name of that accomplice is Chance. Chance always marched along with Bonaparte.

Had he any views, any theories of his own? Yes, no doubt, when he was a young man. They quitted him one by one, or he quitted them, as he came to know more and more of life. The great thing was that he kept his eyes open, he noted and remembered, he was ready for any emergency. In the beginning, a pupil at the École Brienne, a King's scholar, an officer at sixteen, the love of Corsica was in his very bones. It was Corsica first and the rest nowhere. Luckily for him, his native land rejected him. Back he went to France, but without any love for it. He would as soon have served the Grand Turk (as a matter of fact he twice had an idea of going and reorganizing the Sultan's army). He did a lot of reading in his subaltern's quarters; Rousseau, whose *Contrat Social* filled him with delight, the Abbé Raynal, the Comte de Guibert's technical works on artillery, and the Encyclopaedists, and Corneille, too, and the Latins. We have a little novel from his pen, somewhat in the style of *Héloise*, speeches in which he draws an emphatic contrast between the pleasure-seekers and 'those ambitious, pale-faced young men who turn the world upside down'. 'The pale-faced ambitious young man' was himself. But we must not leave out of the account this passion for reading and writing. As Balzac well observes, many a great man began by being a man of letters. For that career, Bonaparte was thoroughly equipped, and when, later on, he came to 'compose' his life and turn it into a legend, a stupendous romance he made of it, well-calculated to fire the imagination.

A series of chances, seized deliberately, with an almost invariably unerring instinct, soon enabled the pale and ambitious one to lay a grip on Fortune. To start with, Toulon was in revolt and had called in the aid of the English. Young Captain Bonaparte had the task of helping to reduce the place. He knew the town's weak spot, and it was largely owing to him that it surrendered. He was promoted brigadier-general and, in 1794, he was appointed to command the artillery with the army serving in Italy. He became a close friend of the younger Robespierre and joined the Jacobins. That, unfortunately, was just before the 9th Thermidor. He was arrested, and then released. He was offered a command in Vendée and refused it. Very soon afterwards the chance of chances came his way. On the 12th Vendémiaire, the Assembly appointed Barras to take the necessary measures for its defence against the royalist insurgents in Paris. Barras requested that he might have General Bonaparte to assist him. On the 13th Vendémiaire, Bonaparte crushed the attempt at counter-revolution on the steps of Saint-Roch.

He was twenty-seven years of age. He had just married a Creole who had seen a good deal of life, and looked it. She had probably been Barras's mistress, and was six years Bonaparte's senior. Her name was Joséphine de Beauharnais. He was appointed Commander-in-Chief of the Army in Italy. And so off he went on that dazzling campaign, a festival of youth and gaiety. Later on, we find Stendhal vaunting his everlasting 'alacrity'. He made peace, without consulting the Directory, and his peace was as novel and original as his war. He returned to Paris covered with glory. Here was the man to ensure a victorious peace! But the East began to call him, the East which always obsessed his imagination, for he was still a man of letters, and a politician to boot. What he longed to do was to deal a blow at England, the Arch-enemy, by way of Suez, Egypt and the Indies. He sets out for Egypt, plays the Sultan there awhile and pushes on as far as Judea, is deeply moved by the religious associations of the place, creates modern Egypt in his stride, grows desperate at what he hears of Joséphine's perfidy, learns to despise both men and women, con-fesses that Rousseau fills him with disgust and that primitive man — the East had told him this — was not born good. Then he went off again, disguising his semi-reverse in Egypt as an honourable retreat. In 1799, he returned again to France and, to his surprise, was hailed as a hero. He did not know that the game was up there, and that he was their sole resource.

THE 18TH BRUMAIRE

War abroad, rioting and discontent at home. Sieyès one of the later Directors, an ex-priest and a regicide, saw — and he was the only one who did see — that there would have to be a big change-over if the essential principles of the Revolution were to be upheld. With him, he had not only (as people think) the adversaries of the Republic, but also a goodly number of its sup-porters. No doubt transforming the Constitution, turning out the deputies, calling in this general who was hand-in-glove with Barras, meant running the risk of a military dictatorship. But better that than the return of the Bourbons — at least so thought the regicides.

The plot was engineered by Sieyès and backed up by the intellectuals. Cabanis stood by Bonaparte, and on the eve of the great Brumaire affair, the victorious general went to call on Madame Helvetius, the widow of the illustrious philosopher. Sick of the Republic, but not of the Revolution, Sieyès and his friends were drifting back to Voltaire and the Encyclopaedists, judging that the only thing to save them from a restoration of the old, traditional monarchy was another 'enlightened despotism'.

Nevertheless, the whole thing nearly went awry, and all owing to Bonaparte. Here again the philosophy of chance would have a good deal to be said for it, and it is curious to observe, when the decisive day arrived, how the man of genius not only did nothing, but did not know what to do, and the others had to bear the brunt.

The 18th Brumaire — the 9th November, 1799, — the Council of Ancients was summoned on the pretext of some imaginary plot. They immediately passed a resolution removing the Corps Législatif to Saint Cloud and appointing Bonaparte to command the Paris garrison. This preliminary operation went off almost without a hitch.

By the 19th — fancy arranging a *coup d'état* in two instalments! — the Councils had had time to think things over. Sieyès's supporters, moderate men for the most part, were nonplussed by their adversaries' tactics. The intellectuals wavered at the thought of defying the powers that be. As Albert Vandal admirably put it, 'The Institute looked like bungling its *coup d'état*'.

The soldiers nearly bungled theirs, even more completely. Bonaparte, to begin with, put in an appearance before the Council of Ancients, who had just had notice brought them that the Directory had resigned, in order to demand a new constitution. His speech was not a success. With the Five Hundred, he fared worse. 'Down with the Dictator!' they cried. 'Down with the Tyrant!' 'Outlaw!' Getting clear of that tumult as best he could, he mounted his charger to harangue his wavering troops. He seemed like a man recovering from a swoon. His face was all covered with bleeding scratches, which he had given himself in his agitation. He shouted out that an attempt had been made to assassinate him.

The situation was entirely saved by Napoleon's brother, Lucien Bonaparte, president of the Five Hundred. He warned the conspirators, had himself dragged away from the tribune by ten men and, when he got outside, within hearing of the troops, gave out that the Five Hundred were a lot of murderers in revolt against the Law. Hearing his stirring words, they hesitated no longer. The Grenadiers rushed in and drove the members from the Hall.

Before they left St. Cloud, they came across thirty or forty fleeing legislators in the woods. They rounded them up and, by the light of a few tallow dips, compelled them to vote the appointment of three Consuls. The 18th Brumaire had ended triumphantly.

Next day, the new Constitution did not indulge in any

flourish of trumpets. Sieyès was responsible for it. He drew up a list of notabilities, virtually abolished the sovereignty of the people, as well as public and parliamentary liberties. At the apex of his pyramid, Sieyès put a Grand Elector, whose duty it was to appoint two Consuls, one for peace and the other for war. Bonaparte refused the post of Grand Elector. They then fell back on the idea of three Consuls, one of whom should have precedence of the other two. He was, of course, the young general. The second Consul was a moderate regicide named Cambacérès. The third, Lebrun, was one of Maupéou's secretaries, a representative of that 'revolution' which, under Louis XV, had aimed a blow at the Parliaments. The selection of such diverse elements to form a government was significant. As for the mob, for ten years now they had been voting this and voting that, and they were sick of it. And the intellectuals were sick of the mob and their caprices. Thus, after so many years of the Republic, men came back to the Revolution, in its moderate form, and to the 'enlightened despotism' of the eighteenth century.

It was with the Consulship that Napoleon Bonaparte attained to the supreme power we call a dictatorship. His first step was to restore confidence, to bring back money into the country, to reinstate old taxes under new names, and to create the Bank of France. He reorganized the constitution by setting up prefects, non-elective, as the direct representatives of the government. Such were the institutions of the Year VIII, the framework of modern France as we know it to-day. The principles of the Revolution still remained in force. The receivers of national property still had their guarantees. Finally, Bonaparte tried to bring off his great fusion. He summoned new men to take office, but he summoned some old ones as well. Before long he installed himself at the Tuileries, and had the *émigrés* recalled.

Abroad, it appeared he was fulfilling his mission of conquest and pacification. In 1800, came Marengo; in 1802 he signed the peace of Amiens, resumed diplomatic relations with the Papacy and set up the Concordat. Already he had discarded the anti-clerical policy of the Revolution. But this was in order to resume the protection of the traditional religion. Incidentally, he concerned himself with the Protestants and granted a statute to the Jews. But he did all these things as one who was master of the situation, who could give, or withhold, at pleasure. A *Te Deum* was sung at Notre-Dame; Bonaparte had himself appointed Consul for life. Ere long we shall find him taking steps to entrench himself still more securely.

By way of introduction, there must needs be a crime. That crime was the assassination of the Duc d'Enghien. Napoleon always accepted complete responsibility for the deed, and described it as a sacrifice necessary for his safety and his career. Once Enghien was shot, Napoleon had given the supreme pledge to the partisans of the Revolution; he had ranged himself with the regicides. The day after the murder, a member of the Tribunal, one Curée, exclaimed, 'Bonaparte has taken sides with the Convention'. The remark was a pregnant one. It was this same Curée who proposed the re-establishment

of the monarchy under the high-sounding name of
Empire and in the person of Napoleon Bonaparte. Had
it not been for that grave at Vincennes, the Empire
would have been impossible. Never would the Republicans have endured it, any more than they would have
endured the Concordat. We must never lose sight of
this policy of *quid pro quo*.

Napoleon had now reached the pinnacle of his glory,
his Coronation, the Pope coming from Rome to anoint
the little Corsican usurper with the sacred oil and gird
his brow with the crown of Charlemagne.

And yet, even now, a keen eye could have discerned
some cracks in the edifice. War was still going on.
Austerlitz, well and good — but then there was Trafalgar,
where the French fleet had been completely annihilated.
At Tilsitt, peace was concluded with Russia. Never
shone the sun so fairly on this youthful Empire. Nevertheless, things looked ominous in Spain, where Napoleon
had set up one of his brothers. There was a rising in
Prussia. Henceforth the wheel of Fortune seemed to
revolve with growing swiftness. Joséphine having been
cast off, the Corsican, anxious to safeguard his position,
becomes the son-in-law of the Caesars by espousing
Marie Louise, granddaughter of Marie Antoinette and
Louis XVI, and daughter of the Emperor of Austria.
In 1811, a son was born to him, a son who in time to
come was to have been lord of this vast dominion with
its hundred and thirty departments, stretching from the
Tiber to the Elbe and comprising the Kingdom of Italy,

Switzerland and the vassal states. But the Muscovite alliance came to an end and Bonaparte set forth on his ill-fated Russian campaign. In Paris it was reported that he was dead. During the few hours that General Malet's conspiracy lasted, no one so much as remembered there was such a person in existence as Napoleon II. No, Napoleon had not founded a dynasty. It was an ominous sign, this!

Then came the *débacle*, the campaign in France, a magnificent but fruitless effort, the revolt of the Marshals, the abdication of the 7th April, 1814. The tale was told, the Emperor had vanished; there remained but a petty princeling relegated to an island in the Mediterranean. Louis XVIII re-entered Paris.

We need not record how, one fine day in the springtime, the forgotten one came back to life, how he escaped from Elba, where he had been passing his time in organizing everything anew, and how, landing at the Gulf of Juan he made his way to Paris. Then, as before, his rallying cry was the Revolution. Summoning the working classes and the peasantry to his side, he bade them make war on the oppressors, and marched forward to the cry of 'Down with the priests! Down with the nobles!' Europe closed its ranks once more. This final adventure was to last but a hundred days, despite his concessions to the Republicans, despite a further addition to the constitutions of the Empire, a half-hearted charter of liberty.

He abdicated and surrendered himself to the English, even as Themistocles surrendered himself to the Persian King. It was a striking act, the sort of thing one reads of in books, and it leads us to look on him as one who was fain to dramatize his destiny. He was sent into exile at St. Helena, where he crowned his stupendous and premeditated story with the sufferings of martyrdom and the composition of his legend. 'My martyrdom', said he, 'is the only thing that can restore the crown to my descendants.' He died, one wild night of storm, on the 5th May, 1821.

He bequeathed to posterity the most amazing memory that man has ever had to dazzle his imagination withal. Poets and ballad-mongers set busily to work on his legend, till, a few years later, it again became incarnate in another Napoleon, the third of the name. The defeat that befell this later Bonaparte will never dim the fascination that dwells in the countenance of his predecessor. The story of Napoleon, the champion of might, will always remain a myth that everyone will interpret according to his own ideas.

He was the most transcendently impressive of all dictators that have ever been. He himself has said, with his incomparable insight, that his power was 'all imagination'. And it is a fact that dictators must appeal to the imagination if they would reap success. According to some, Napoleon was an organizer of genius, while others will have it (we read it in the official proclamations of his descendants) that he was the Republic personified. That he loved power, there is no denying. He declared that he loved it 'like an artist', as a musician loves his violin. Yet it is very certain that he tried to preserve the most characteristic fruits of the Revolution, and that, apart from his concern for public order, he did perpetuate its most conspicuous results.

He is one of the most perfect examples of dictator, because dictatorship, which is almost invariably based on social aspirations, retains some of their elements though it inscribes them in a severe and rigorous form; because a dictator, as soon as he settles down, has always as his essential idea the fusion of past and present, provided his rule is uncontested.

Lastly, he is the typical dictator because he was aware of a dictator's limitations. He was always saying that his dynasty was not old enough, and that he was powerless to counteract that disability. General Malet's conspiracy made it clear to him that his son would not reign after him. He made an immense effort to consolidate his power, to endeavour to make it operative beyond the grave — the grave which is the inexorable bourne of all dictatorships. He nearly succeeded, and that by the strangest device, and one least susceptible of definition — by poetry. He made himself Emperor of the soul. It was his last card, and, since in 1831 the King of Rome, the Duke of Reichstadt, died obscurely in Austria, the card was taken up by his nephew, the son of Hortense de Beauharnais and Louis of Holland. True, the game was lost in 1870, but Napoleon Bonaparte did all a dictator could to ensure the permanence of his dynasty, all, and more than all that mortal man could do.

And still to-day he is, and will never cease to be, the most astounding being that has ever issued from the commonalty and risen to be its leader. And yet, looking at the upshot of it all, did he not say himself, with the inexorable sense of reality which never left him, that it had been better had he never been born?

NAPOLEON III

IT may be due to the intrinsic poetry of the Napoleonic legend that nineteenth-century France, whose annals had been inaugurated by the most famous dictatorship of all time, was led to revive that form of government and to call it an Empire. The Bourbons had restored peace to the country and re-established its finances on a sound basis. In spite of an abnormally sensitive public opinion, which, with Monsieur Thiers as its mouthpiece, urged war against England on account of Spain, Belgium or Egypt, Louis-Philippe had kept the peace at home and in Europe generally. But that state of affairs was not calculated to satisfy men who had lived through great convulsions, and still less their sons. Lamartine summed up the situation in a somewhat mischievous phrase. 'France', he said 'is bored'. It is true that prosperity is boring. But it was not for long, life was soon to become entertaining and picturesque enough.

Thanks to the printed matter that originated at Saint Helena, thanks to ballads, romances, legends, poems, to Hugo and Béranger, the Napoleonic legend was complete. The frail Austrian Archduke — the Man's son — was no more. He had died at the age of twenty. In whom, henceforth, were the Bonapartists to place their hopes?

According to the rules which Napoleon himself had laid down, it was the eldest son of Louis and Hortense who was to succeed to the Crown. Like his brother, young Napoleon was an enthusiast for new ideas. He may have thought of looking out for a throne in Italy. Both of them became Carbonari and conspired against the Pope. In 1831 the insurrection of the Papal States almost succeeded, but the elder brother was killed by a bullet through the heart, in the Apennines. His brother Louis became heir to the Empire.

He was little more than a boy, of soft and dreamy disposition, a wholehearted admirer of the founder of the dynasty and, it might have been thought, hardly fitted to succeed to such a heritage. Fortunately there was his mother. Said Cardinal Consalvi to the Pope one day:

'There was only one man in Napoleon's family and he's locked up. Now there's no one.'

'There's Queen Hortense,' said Pius VII.

It was this amiable, pleasure-loving but extraordinarily intelligent woman and, apparently, even more of a Creole than her mother Joséphine, who was destined to restore the Empire. Her son had written (they were always great writers in that family) an *Artillery Manual*, *Poetical Reveries* and *Thoughts on Switzerland*. He had kept in touch with the leading Bonapartists and the Republicans, who were united in a common hatred of the Bourbons and the Orleanists. One day he considered the hour had come. He had won over a Colonel at Strasbourg, thought the garrison was with him and made his appearance in the city. He was immediately arrested. Hortense besought her friends to intervene, Madame Récamier in particular. In a tactful but rather humiliating way for him, the Pretender was given his freedom.

He set sail for America, whence he returned just in

time to witness the death of the mother to whom he owed
so much. The political testament which Hortense left
behind her is a masterpiece of bold common sense.
'The proper line for the Bonapartes to take', said she,
'is to make out that they are everybody's friends. They
are the mediators . . . We must never weary of affirming
that the Emperor was infallible and that he had the
country's interests at heart in all he did. If you say a
thing often enough, people come to believe it. In France
you can always get the best of an argument by appealing
to History. No one reads it and everyone believes in it
. . . As I have told you: look well ahead. There's not
a comedy or a drama going on under your eyes that
doesn't give you a chance of intervening like a *deus ex
machina*.' Finally 'The world can easily be caught twice
with the same bait.' And that is just what happened.
Exiled to England after the death of Hortense, Louis
Napoleon, in 1839, published his *Idées Napoléoniennes*, in
which he speaks of the founder of his dynasty as of a god.
In this work he sums up the gist of his ideas: Peace to be
established in Europe by observing the principle of
nationality in the delimitation of frontiers; adjustment
of the claims of liberty and authority, the distribution of
land not under cultivation, the working-class to be free
to own land, freedom of trade. All this was at the very
time when Prince de Joinville was bringing Napoleon's
ashes back to France. Surely this was the right moment
if any was. He landed at Boulogne, a plucked eagle on
his shoulder, and was arrested even more promptly than
at Strasbourg. It looked as if he would be laughed off the
stage. It was the rigour of his sentence that saved him.

In the fortress of Ham in which he was imprisoned, the Imperial pretender settled down to work. He wrote on the abolition of poverty, the Nicaraguan canal, electricity, sugar-beet and artillery. Six years in prison gave him ample leisure to think out his schemes, and they were numerous. In 1846, learning that his father was dying, he planned his escape. He managed it, simply enough. He got away from the fortress of Ham in a blouse lent him by a working mason called Badinguet and this was how the nephew of the great Emperor came to be known for the rest of his days as 'Badinguet'.

Matters took a turn that facilitated his rise to power. In 1848 the monarchy came to an end and France was once more a Republic. Louis Napoleon stood as a candidate for the presidency and was elected, five and a half million votes out of a total of seven million being recorded in his favour.

His task was now to restore the Empire. It took him three whole years to make up his mind to attempt it. On the whole, he was pretty satisfied with his rise to power. It had been rapid enough. Moreover, he had sworn to uphold the Constitution, and felt some qualms about going back on his word. However, the Assembly mistrusted him, refusing either to augment his civil list or to amend the law so as to permit of his re-election. It was this that put it into his head to try and coerce the deputies, most of whom, be it observed, were monarchists, but, as they were divided into two camps, Legitimists and Orleanist, they had been unable to come to an agreement.

The *coup d'état* of the 2nd December, 1851, is a

standing model of what a Governmental *coup d'état* should be. The men who accomplished it were Persigny and, more particularly, Morny, who was reputed to be an illegitimate son of General de Flahaut and Queen Hortense, and consequently the future Emperor's own half-brother. Every precaution was taken to keep the matter secret. The eve of the day fixed for the attempt was the anniversary of Austerlitz, and the Prince-President was giving an evening reception at the Elysée. Neither Morny nor Persigny put in an appearance. They arrived later on, when all the guests had departed. The Prince assigned them their respective roles. Morny was to have the Interior, Persigny was told off to occupy the Palais-Bourbon, General de Saint-Arnaud to see about enforcing martial law, and M. de Maupas was to arrest some of the recalcitrants, notably Cavaignac and Thiers.

Next morning. Louis Napoleon rode forth on his charger, accompanied by Saint-Arnaud and the aged King Jérôme, Napoleon's brother, with whom he had recently been reconciled. He rode all through Paris, and back again to his official residence, acclaimed nearly everywhere by cheering crowds. Word was brought to him that two hundred and twenty deputies had been incarcerated in the d'Orsay barracks. Of legal resistance there had been none. Next day the Deputies of the Left attempted to put up barricades. Repressive measures were rather severe, and the stories of 'somewhat rough handling by the police', which were a good deal commented upon, made it look for a time as if things were going to take an ugly turn. Some departments rebelled.

Saint Arnaud, Persigny and Morny thereupon gave orders that they should be sternly dealt with. Martial law was proclaimed in thirty-two departments, a hundred thousand citizens were put under arrest, and eighty-four deputies expelled.

On the 20th December, a popular referendum, by seven and a half million votes to six hundred thousand, declared in favour of Louis Napoleon Bonaparte and appointed him President for ten years. The dictator was firmly established.

One year later, after a skilful campaign of speechifying, and the constant repetition of the slogan 'Empire means Peace', the President assumed the title of Emperor. Once more the Republic had departed.

Throughout the eighteen years of his reign Napoleon had two predominant aims in view. First his energies were directed towards bringing his own social and humanitarian ideas to pass, and secondly to establishing his dynasty on a firm basis. Abroad, he upheld his famous nationalistic policy, took a hand in setting up the Kingdom of Italy, intrigued, none too adroitly, in Germany, and, together with Bismarck, who played the part of Simple Simon, pursued the vain *politique de pourboires*, with the result that, at the end of his reign, he found himself without a single ally. Finally, he engaged his military forces in the disastrous Mexican adventure, hoping to establish an Empire there in favour of Maximilian of Austria. To his credit, it must be recorded that, in 1860, owing to his efforts, Savoy and Nice were once more reunited with France.

At home, the Empire pursued a complicated policy.

The Civil Service, ably reorganized on Napoleonic lines, worked on the whole smoothly and well. The 1867 Exhibition seems to register the high-water mark of the new régime, which was now almost unanimously recognized. The opposition of the Republicans and the Exiles, of whom the most notable was Victor Hugo, was without effect.

Rochefort's epigrams, though celebrated among the Parisians, found scarcely an echo in the provinces. The Empire stood firm, but the crowned dictator had misgivings about himself and his reign. He began to get more and more fatalistic in his ideas, and ill-health was sapping his vitality.

A jesting remark of his throws a revealing light on his state of mind. 'How can you expect things to go smoothly? The Empress is a Legitimist, I am a Republican. Persigny is the only Bonapartist among us.'

When it was decided to mitigate the absolutism of a régime where freedom of the press was non-existent, where there was no real parliamentary system, it was generally thought that a liberal Empire following on a despotic one would be sure to have more stability. The plébiscite of 1870 afforded further proof to Napoleon that the country was with him. Three months later, Bismarck's manœuvres had succeeded, and France and Prussia were at war. Ill-armed, ill-prepared though she was, France rushed blindly into hostilities. At Sedan, the second Napoleonic dictatorship ended in a disaster the magnitude of which made dictatorships unpopular in France for many a day to come.

Nevertheless Napoleon III's example and experience

were not without their lesson for future dictators. He had relied on the votes of the masses, as against the parliamentary system, and the masses had backed him up. Plébiscite and dictatorship are synonymous expressions. In 1889, when his turn came, General Boulanger nearly succeeded in getting himself voted into power, but he omitted to gain control of the army while the Paris mob was for him. His attempt was a failure. And so we may say that, for France at all events, and so far as our present experience goes, if revolutions are born in the street, *coups d'état* are merely repetitions of the 18th Brumaire and the 2nd December, that is to say, they are organized inside the government by those who are already in power. That is almost axiomatic and it were well to bear it in mind.

A HISTORY
BRIEF BUT ASTONISHING
OF THE
SOUTH AMERICAN REPUBLICS

LATIN America has always been the happy hunting ground for dictators, or for what a Venezuelan writer has described as 'democratic imperialism'. If it were possible to go back far enough into the past, and if the history of the ages that preceded Columbus were freed from the unsubstantial hypotheses that too often encumber it, we should doubtless readily perceive that, well before the arrival of the Spaniards and the Portuguese, the great empires established by their predecessors were founded on individual government of a kind which, contrary to what the earliest historians of the period have assumed, was nearly always opposed to hereditary monarchy.

It is not our intention to go back to those remote ages in which truth and fable are intermingled. As with all the peoples of the earth, the races of Southern and Central America had their eponymous heroes, half-mythical beings who appear to have exercised what we in these days should call a dictatorship, except that we must add to the ordinary meaning of the word a certain religious implication. Thus the Aztecs, whose imposing Empire extended from the Yucatan peninsula over the whole of Mexico, recognized Tenoch as the heroic founder of their nation, that Tenoch who died in the middle of the fourteenth century. It may have been to Tenoch that they owed their constitution, a signally cruel one be it noted, which had to adapt itself as best it could to the rule of a single supreme head. It was under his leadership that the little tribe of Aztecs succeeded in making themselves masters of the rich cities which had sprung up since the seventh century, and they attained the pinnacle of their greatness under Montezuma the Great, the first of his name. The fact that, later on, there was a second Montezuma, dear to the folk of the seventeenth century as being the victim of the Spaniards, has led some people to infer that there was a dynasty of this name. The truth is that the dynastic idea never appealed to the Mexican leaders, and some writers claim that their policy bore a much closer resemblance to the Bonapartist dictatorship, inasmuch as it was a government at once monarchical, elective and popular, with a Council of Notables and Elders playing the part of a Senate or House of Peers.

But the Aztecs were not the only people to afford an example of a rigidly organized society. The Mayas of Central America, the Aymaras and Quichuas of Bolivia and Peru, were governed on more or less similar lines. Present-day ethnologists detect among them some striking prototypes of the modern Marxist constitution. It was in the eleventh century that the Empire of the Incas was founded in Peru by the Children of the Sun, Manco Capac and his sister Manco Huaco, on the ruins of the Empire of the Aymaras. The land was divided into portions and the State was organized on strictly communistic lines. This did not prevent the Chiefs, or Incas (there were two of them, one temporal, the other religious) from occupying a privileged position and possessing half the soil, which was cultivated by a downtrodden proletariat.

When the Spaniards arrived on the scene, the struggle

upon which they forthwith entered with the various autochthonous powers was not, as people in the eighteenth century erroneously believed, a struggle between an oppressed and inoffensive people who loved their freedom and a sanguinary foe. It was a war to the knife between nations equally proud, between two civilizations both of them based on force. It is eminently necessary to master this plain truth, if we are to arrive at a more or less clear idea of the subsequent stages of American history, which legend and contending passions have so largely bedimmed. Popular government, in the liberal sense we give the term, was never able to gain a footing in these countries, whether in their autonomous days or when they were under the heel of the European conqueror, or even later on, when they had won their independence. Save in the case of Brazil, and then only temporarily, they never produced a dynasty, but were always being pitchforked to and fro from one dictator to another. Nor did they come to realize the blessings of peace until the central government, cruel and unjust as it sometimes was, was strong enough to impose it. This is the lesson to be learnt from the history of the different nationalities of America.

MEXICO

MEXICO, thanks to the high degree of civilization achieved by the Aztecs, was a powerfully organized state when the Spaniards arrived on the scene. Their leader in those days was Montezuma II who, encouraging his subjects to pay him divine honours, dissipated the state treasure and ground down his people by crushing taxation. There was nothing in him of the romantic hero to whom our philosophers lent such widespread popularity. When Fernando Cortez invaded his territory, the Spanish Conquistador was quick to make capital out of the jealousies and hatreds which the tyrant had engendered. Cortez made himself master of Mexico, and Montezuma was taken prisoner. One day, when he essayed to interpose between the invaders and his subjects in an attempt to persuade the latter to abandon the conflict, he was overwhelmed with a shower of arrows and stones, and perished. The date of his death was 30th June, 1520. So far is he from exciting the veneration of his countrymen, that his memory to-day is reviled by the Mexicans, who look on him as a traitor. Reputations are as unstable as popular opinion.

The hero of the fruitless struggle for independence, the Mexican Vercingetorix, a gigantic statue of whom adorns the principal square of Mexico city, then a young man of twenty-five, was Cuauhtemoc, the *Eagle that descended*, who, in Europe, is also known as Guatimozin. Guatimozin succeeded in rallying round him as one man all the divers nations which had formerly owed fealty to the Aztecs. Cortez conquered Mexico, and Guatimozin yielded himself his prisoner, as Vercingetorix had surrendered to Caesar. At first he was treated with some consideration, but later on, in order to wrest from him the secret of the royal treasures, Cortez had put him to the torture, and finally hanged him. He is looked upon to-day as the most illustrious hero of the national fight for freedom, and the first who made Mexico a united nation. It may be so, but we have no facts to prove it.

On the government of the invaders, who gave the country the name of New Spain, there is no need for us to dilate. It has been judged severely and with unnecessary passion It seems only too well established that the conquerors were guilty of many atrocities. But, before long, the first batch of Franciscan monks arrived, took the Indians under their protection, built schools and hospitals and began a wonderful work of civilization. Among a rather mixed collection, some of the viceroys stand out as humane and noble figures. Such were Antonio de Mendoza, Luis de Velasco, emancipator of the Indians, and Archbishop Payo de Rivera. It must be observed that these viceroys enjoyed almost unlimited powers and were virtually free of all control, so long as the mines furnished the requisite quantity of silver to the Madrid government. Honour, then, or the reverse, is due to them for the measures which, as all-powerful proconsuls, they took with regard to the country committed to their charge.

At the beginning of the nineteenth century, the propaganda of the French Encyclopaedists, who had picked out Spain, the Spain of the monks and the Inquisition, as a symbol of every depravity of which the human mind is capable, began to bear fruit in Mexico. The example of the French Revolution, the knowledge that the legitimate dynasty, the Bourbons, had been ousted from Madrid in order to make room for Joseph Bonaparte, the scandalous quarrels between Charles IV and his son Ferdinand, all combined to create a ferment in the public mind and to prepare it for the idea of Mexican independence.

It was a village curé, Miguel Hidalgo by name, who on the 16th September, 1810, raised the standard of revolt and proclaimed the autonomy of his country.

With regard to the curé Hidalgo, history speaks with two voices. For some, he was a national hero, the most glorious star in the annals of Mexico, next after Guatimozin. For others he was a knave, a cunning opportunist, a sordid practitioner of repulsive vices. Passions always run high when it is the early history of Spanish America that is in question.

He was of Spanish origin, curé of the little village of Dolores. It is an established fact that he planted mulberry trees for the purpose of rearing silkworms, and such bucolic activities have never failed to warm republican hearts. The government, proudly tenacious of the reputation of Spanish silks, had the mulberry trees destroyed. Then Don Miguel planted vines, which suffered a similar fate.

At this time, a woman of Queretaro, Doña Josefa Ortiz, was fomenting a conspiracy. Hidalgo joined forces with her in order to put an end to the ill-treatment meted out to his mulberry trees. Doña Josefa, however, was denounced, and, on her arrest, Hidalgo proclaimed the independence of Mexico. At that time he had with him only a few officers and ten men armed with sabres. His proclamation is known under the name of the *Cry of Dolores*.

The day being a Sunday, he had the bell rung for Mass and brought together his little flock, who decided to follow him. Then he marched from village to village shouting 'Long live Our Lady of Guadelupe and death to the Spaniards ' The curé shortly proclaimed himself Captain-General, scored a few successes, though he failed to reduce Mexico, and ordered the abolition of slavery throughout the land, under pain of death. That decree, incidentally, was never put into execution.

Unfortunately, if we are to credit other historians, this poor Mexican edition of the Vicaire Savoyard was in the enjoyment of an annual income amounting to four hundred thousand francs and all his aims and ideas were directed towards establishing a sort of demagogic theocracy over Mexico, of which he was to be the sovereign lord. He represented himself as the champion of a downtrodden peasantry, but he gave fêtes on a royal scale, at which his mistress did the honours.

Be that as it may, on the 17th January, 1811, the royalists routed the hordes of the revolutionary curé at Calderon, and Hidalgo was shot on the 1st August of the same year.

Another curé, whose character is also the subject of

dispute, succeeded him: this was Don José Maria Morelos y Pavon. He was possessed of some military talent and inflicted on the royalists (who were not all Europeans but counted some worthy Mexicans among their number) a series of minor defeats. His chief lieutenants bore imposing names. One was called Bravo, and the other Matamoros.

The curé Morelos again proclaimed the independence of Mexico (which, perhaps, was not very thoroughly convinced of it) and decreed the abolition of slavery. Unhappily he is accused of establishing, under another name, a sort of Inquisition more cruel than its predecessor and of framing laws against foreigners, who were forbidden to sojourn in America because they imperilled 'the purity of the Blessed Virgin'. Without presuming to decide between these conflicting interpretations, we will merely add that, like the curé Hidalgo, the curé Morelos was taken prisoner and shot, in 1813.

The religious and social activities of these two revolutionaries are, it must be confessed, far removed from the ideas of the French Revolution. They are much more Spanish in colour, and, as we have seen, much rather the dictates of faith than of reason. In any case it is well to observe that, between the armies of the Viceroy and the hordes of the two curés, there was no difference of blood. The wars of independence were civil wars, in which Mexicans on either side of the barricade, or the altar, took part. The explanation is that the affair at bottom was much more social than political, a truth that these *ad hoc* dictators had clearly recognized.

The domestic dissensions in Spain did not fail to have

a corresponding effect on Mexico. Part of the population accepted the liberal and rationalistic Constitution of Ferdinand VII, while others rejected it and clamoured for the return of the Jesuits. The higher clergy thereupon espoused the cause of freedom, a plan for a rising was drawn up, in which the freemasons forbade their members to take part, on pain of death. To-day they take to themselves all the credit for bringing about the liberation of Mexico.

In reality the war was carried on by Colonel Iturbide, to whom all the towns flung wide their gates. Unfortunately Iturbide, when the victory was won, was loath to offer the crown of an independent Mexico to a Bourbon. He proclaimed himself Emperor, and the freemasons, aided and abetted by the Anglo-Saxons, dethroned and shot him in 1823. A federal Republic, modelled on the Republic of the United States of North America, was now proclaimed. It involved a whole series of struggles and civil conflicts in which military *coups d'état* followed on the *pronunciamentos*. Certain States declared their independence. In 1857, Mexico proclaimed the separation of Church and State, nationalized ecclesiastical property, and suspended payment of the external debt. It was at this juncture that Napoleon III undertook the disastrous Mexican campaign, with the object of providing the Archduke Maximilian of Austria with an Imperial throne.

Almost immediately, matters took an ill turn. The forces of the country rallied as one man about an Indian, Benito Juarez, who, at twelve years of age, did not even know his letters. Juarez defeated Maximilian at Queretaro in 1867 and put him to death. Thereafter he remained in power until his death, which occurred five years later. To secure his position, he had to employ considerable severity and he was unable to put down the civil wars which were constantly breaking out between the opposing parties, the United States and the freemasons. His successor met with no better fortune.

It was not until the year 1877 that Mexico reached a period of relative prosperity under the rule of its most famous and its only beneficent dictator. Porfirio Diaz had borne arms against the United States and had attained the rank of general. When, at the age of forty-seven, he was elected President of the Republic, there was not a piastre in the State Treasury. By the time he had completed three years of office, Porfirio had reorganized the civil service, established friendly relations with the foreign powers, built railways, introduced the telegraph and constructed roads. This was all very fine, and his successor, General Gonsalez, fired with the fever of emulation embarked on a policy of public works on such a scale that it soon brought Mexico to ruin. In 1884, Porfirio Diaz was hastily recalled to power. He at once proceeded to subject the financial laws and methods to a strict revision, raised a loan, introduced cuts into the salaries of public servants and reduced the subsidies paid to the railways. Meantime he pursued his public works scheme. As a result of his prudence it was soon found possible progressively to restore the cuts that had been necessitated by the crisis, and Mexico was at last enabled to enjoy a period of genuine prosperity.

Needless to say, Porfirio Diaz was re-elected President several times.

But men are mortal, and personal governments do not outlast the life of a man. When its most famous leader disappeared, Mexico relapsed once more into a welter of intestine quarrels and upheavals. It does not look as if an issue out of its afflictions were yet in sight.

However, Porfirio Diaz's experiment may be looked on as a new departure. He had shown us the spectacle of an engineer-economist acting the part of dictator. His was a scientific and, to some extent, a technocratic dictatorship, carried out in a country which had seen but little change since the days of the Conquistadores. It surely proves that nothing is to be dismissed as impossible.

SOUTH AMERICA

THE history of South America under the Spanish domination exhibits, in its early stages, a marked resemblance to that of Mexico. We have the same excesses on the part of the conquerors, the same importation of negroes in order to supply the deficiency of the autochthonous population, the same organization, and, be it added, the same subsequent diversity of opinion in regard to the interpretation of the facts. It is well established that the Jesuits, at all events in Paraguay, where they set up the semi-communist organization of the Reductions, extended their protection to the Guarani Indians, and definitely founded the civilized Christian communities of South America. A few of the Viceroys also succeeded in imparting a certain degree of prosperity to some regions despite defective administration. It must be inferred that all was not so ill under the Spanish rule since, at the time of the wars of independence, the struggle was carried on by the inhabitants of the country much more than by the soldiers sent out from Europe. All impartial historians are in agreement on that point to-day, and Simon Bolivar himself confesses in his private letters that he had all his work cut out when, for propaganda purposes, he set about disguising an immense civil war as a war against a foreign invader. During the whole time the conflict was in progress, Spain did not send over more than fifteen thousand men to America. It follows then that to sustain the conflict a large proportion of the colonists must have been genuine royalists. But not until to-day has that fact been recognized.

It was Joseph Bonaparte's arrival in Madrid which, as in Mexico, gave the signal for revolt. Men flew to arms on behalf of Ferdinand VII. Before long, private rivalries intervened and, on the 5th July, 1811, provincial deputies at a meeting at Caracas, proclaimed the independence of Venezuela and the birth of the first republic. And what sort of a republic it was we shall presently discover. Little by little the insurrection spread to the adjoining countries, Chile, Peru and what is now the Argentine. Disorderly hordes of irregulars soon invaded the towns and the country districts. Village curés, fired by what had been taking place in Mexico, stirred up the Indians and the negroes to revolt. Spain was too deeply engaged with her own internal troubles to take action in time. It is true that she was soon to find herself in conflict with a man on the great scale, the real hero of South America, the liberator of a whole continent, Simon Bolivar.

Simon Bolivar was born at Caracas in 1783, and came of a rich family. He had pursued his studies in Madrid and had travelled in Europe and the United States. A widower since his eighteenth year, the outbreak of the Revolution found him living on his own estates. Having become involved in some obscure intrigues, he took refuge at Curaçao where he gathered about him a little army of outlaws, and straightway attempted a blow for the liberation of his country, Venezuela. In 1813, he defeated the royalist Monteverde and took Caracas. He made his entry into the place in a triumphal car drawn by twelve young girls, amid scenes of indescribable enthusiasm. Having consolidated his position by carrying out a few summary executions, he had no sooner assumed the title of dictator of the Western provinces of Venezuela than he began to dream of further conquests.

But to confront him there arose a truculent antagonist, one Boves, who got together an army of *llaneros*, to which he gave the name of the Infernal Legion. It was his aim to wrest the power from Bolivar in order that it might remain in the hands of the Spanish royal house. Boves scored such a decisive victory that Bolivar, compelled to escape in a boat, was obliged to forgo all idea of further progress, until at last Boves was killed in some battle or other. His men gave him a funeral becoming the leader of the Infernal Legion. All the women, children and old men of the town of Uriqua were put to the sword upon his grave.

However, the cause of freedom began to gain ground almost everywhere. The Vice-royalty of Buenos Aires was constituted an independent state. Montevideo, the royalists' last hope, capitulated to the insurgents. Bolivar, at the head of a reorganized army, gained several victories and soon reconquered Venezuela, which was forthwith proclaimed a Republic, one and indivisible. He was presented with a reed with a head of gold at the top as a fitting emblem of supreme authority in a country which could 'bend beneath the wind of adversity but which never broke'.

Moreover, he had just discovered a coadjutor in the person of one who, after himself, is the greatest figure in

Latin America, namely Paez. Paez, like Boves, was a *llanero*. He was indeed an Indian and the idol of the *gauchos* whom he soon rallied to the cause of freedom, though at first they had regarded it but coldly. Astounding stories are related of him: he routed the royalists by loosing herds of wild buffaloes upon them; he flooded the prairies; he captured several gunboats on the great rivers with his men, who plunged on horseback into the deep waters; he could slay as many as forty men with his spear. At the head of his *llaneros* of the Apura plains, Paez soon became the terror of the foes of freedom.

Beneath the banner of Bolivar, who was still an outlaw, everlastingly alternating between victory and flight, men from all the world over — England, France, Scotland — flocked to enrol themselves. He borrowed funds, he eluded his would-be assassins. Despite the undoubted valour of General Morillo, his adversary, Bolivar successfully accomplished the most daring feats. He crossed the Andes during the rains, seized Bogota and, in 1819, founded the Republic of Colombia in union with Venezuela. In 1825, following the example of Chile, Uraguay, Paraguay and Buenos Aires, Peru asserted its independence. Thus, one after another, Spain was losing all her dominions. Among the flags captured from the regiments who were fighting on her side was one that was precious beyond the rest. It was the flag beneath which, three hundred years before, Pizarro had ridden into the capital of the Incas — who now, at long last, had taken their revenge.

After ruling over Peru for a certain time as a dictator, Bolivar returned to Colombia. There he fell under the suspicion of plotting to restore the monarchy for his own purposes. This made him a number of enemies and compelled him to make frequent reference in his speeches to the horror with which the idea of a monarchy inspired him. The truth is that what he really desired was to constitute a federation of South American States, or at least to create a common machinery the more effectively to protect the States in their newly-won freedom. In 1826, he opened a great Congress at Panama, which came to nothing. Bolivar's real plan was doubtless to unite Colombia, Peru, Bolivia, Argentine and Chile in one immense Republic of which he would have been the head, and which would have taken the name of the United States of South America. The Peruvian minister for Foreign Affairs got an inkling of the plan. Paez, who was in command of the military forces of Venezuela, took steps to checkmate Bolivar. The Pan-American Congress proved a failure and a period of mistrust ensued. Peru rejected the Bolivian constitution and Bolivia which, as a mark of gratitude, had assumed the name of the Liberator, now discarded it. A conspiracy nearly robbed him of Colombia. In the end he took his departure and died on the 17th December, 1830, an embittered and disappointed man, having lived long enough to see Colombia split into three separate States: Colombia, Venezuela, and Ecuador.

In him disappeared the greatest Dictator of South America and also its most enigmatic personality. Bolivar has been extolled as the very type and exemplar of a Republican Statesman, whereas it is plain that his lifelong dream was to wield imperial dictatorship over vast

lands. He has been portrayed as a man of humanitarian
ideas deeply imbued with the notions of the eighteenth-
century philosophers, whereas he was in reality a man
of harsh and violent nature who recoiled from no deed
however grim and bloody. Yet, for all his violence he
was, there is no denying it, tender and affectionate in his
private relationships and, in his public life, capable of
kindly and charitable actions. In his general character,
which without doubt bespoke the man of genius, there
was, side by side with the quality that revealed the ob-
server and the dreamer, a truculent *llanero* like Boves or
Paez, a legislator often profound in his insight and a
penetrating student of human nature.

To-day we are beginning to realise that the Colombian
dictator was above all things a positivist, a realist. He
wrote some trenchant things about codes 'drawn up by
gentle visionaries who, dreaming of republics away up
in the clouds, have sought to attain to political perfection
by taking it for granted that human nature is indefinitely
perfectible'. Despite his republican utterances, he was
an uncompromising opponent of democracy, which he
defined as 'a state of things so incapable of resistance that
the slightest difficulty is enough to throw it into confusion
and bring it to naught'.

It would be possible to extract from his recorded say-
ings the sternest possible indictment of parliamentary
government:

'Unlimited freedom, absolute democracy, are reefs
upon which all the republics have come to grief.

'It must never be forgotten that the excellence of a
government consists, not in its theoretic perfection, but

in the degree to which it is adapted to the nature and character of the people for whom it is set up.

'It is not right to leave everything to the chances and hazards of an election. The masses are more prone to error than those who have been trained and tempered by education.

'The shouts of human-kind on the battlefield, or in the tumult of assemblies are protests to heaven against inconsistent legislators who have thought it possible to experiment with chimerical constitutions without suffering the consequences.'

'Absolute democratic government is as much a tyranny as despotism.'

With regard to those who look on Bolivar as a disciple of the French Revolution, we would draw their attention to the following passage: 'The most accomplished nation in the world' he declared, 'ancient or modern, was unable to resist the violence of the storms inherent in pure theories. If a European country like France, ever sovereign and independent, was not able to support the burden of unrestricted liberty, how can anyone expect Colombia to realize the delirious hallucinations of Robespierre and Marat. Could anyone even dream of such a piece of political moonshine? Legislators, see to it that the inexorable verdict of posterity does not liken you to the monsters of France!'

And so Bolivar, being a realist in politics, was always moved to indignation when he saw the States of South America adopting cut and dried constitutions, based on abstract theory, and not created expressly to suit them. What he would have liked to see put into practice was what Latin-American writers have called the Bolivarian theory, that is to say the principle of 'sociocratic heredity' on the Comtean or pre-Comtean pattern. He would have desired, taking his cue no doubt from the example of the Antonines at Rome, that, at the head of each of the Republics he had created, there should be a Life-President, who should appoint his own successor. In this manner he thought to combine absolutism and continuity, the apanage of hereditary monarchies, while discarding the hereditary principle.

Not all of Bolivar's ideas have been put into practice. However, the States that succeeded to his ideal State have gradually gone back to dictators. The dictator in these regions of wide open spaces and horses is the chief of the *llaneros*, the master of the *gauchos*, the *candillo*. The *candillo* (*candillism* has been absorbed into our current vocabulary) is the *führer* or *duce* of the Venezuelans, the Ecuadorians. In every one of the American States there has appeared at one time or another, the monarchy without a crown, of which Bolivar stands as the theoretic exponent, and which several of his pupils and imitators have put into practice.

COLOMBIA

AFTER the departure and subsequent death of Bolivar, the Republic of Colombia, contracted to what is now New Grenada, the supreme control of the State passed into the hands of General Santander who maintained peace. But when he in turn departed and died, civil war again distracted the country and continued as a permanent feature for a quarter of a century. A conservative member, a certain Dr. Osfina, went so far as to maintain that it was as well that all theories should be given a trial, so that the country might have practical experience of the various forms of government. As we may suppose, Colombia did not stint itself in this respect, and marched rapidly along the road to disaster. Two or three ephemeral dictators made a bid to restore order, but one party or another swiftly brought them down. Not until 1880, do we meet with a real Candillo in the person of Doctor Nunez. Dr. Nunez was a liberal; nevertheless he gave his backing to the central government and brought about an economic recovery. The most singular thing about him was that, throughout the fourteen years of his ascendancy, he was hand in glove with the Catholic Church. Nunez himself was an infidel, but he realized that only with the aid of the clergy could he hope to save the country. 'He saw clearly', to quote the words of a Venezuelan author, 'that the sole visible leader of Colombian unity was the Archbishop of Bogota, because in places where the writ of the National Government did not run, His Grace's did. And though he had no faith, or only a nascent one, in divine influence, he had a blind faith in the influence of the Catholic Church, with which he therefore entered into an alliance in order to restore stability and social tranquillity to his country.' Thus he reverted to the ancient constitution of the Incas with its partnership between the secular head or Zaque and the religious head or Lama. 'It was this union of the Zaque and the Lama, re-enacted in the nineteenth century by Nunez and Archbishop Paul, that succeeded in crushing the forces of anarchy and re-establishing law and order.'

Nunez' dictatorship lasted fourteen years, and ended only with his death. Without any possible doubt, those fourteen years were Colombia's Golden Age.

VENEZUELA

VENEZUELA is the land of Bolivar and of the most picturesque of all *candillos*, the one who has been likened to
a Tartar prince, the celebrated Paez who, when he came
to power, had not yet learned to eat his food with a fork.
In Venezuela, the clergy play a less important part than
in Colombia. On the other hand, people there feel very
strongly about equality, and a Caesar risen from the
ranks would be sure to be the hero of the masses.

The astounding thing was that Paez, though a leader
of hordes of undisciplined desperadoes, showed himself
to be a statesman of no common order, a man of the same
kidney, to choose an example from days long past, as
Robert Guiscard in Southern Italy. Out of the appalling
chaos produced by the civil war, Paez strove, from the
day he was elected President in 1831, to bring forth a
nation. Re-elected, or called back to power, time after
time, this rude faction fighter who, with his *llaneros* had
stirred up a whole people to fight for freedom and then
put all his energies into the separatist movement which
sundered Venezuela from Colombia, turned his country
into the most civilized of the South American States.
He promptly routed the remaining supporters of Colombian unity and forthwith addressed himself to the task
of re-organizing the country's finances. Side by side with
him, an active and ambitious Minister of the Interior,
one Rojas, supported him with sound advice. Unfortunately the quarrels stirred up by his adversaries, and

even by his friends who were jealous of his power, and a federalist civil conflict proved his undoing. Living in exile in New York, he died as recently as 1873, at the age of eighty-three.

Under his successors, of whom the most important was Falcon, the country was a long time in regaining its tranquillity. Despite the attractiveness of the semi-barbarian figure of the *gaucho* Paez, it cannot be denied that Venezuela had no very lively appreciation of its national interests and of less extremist ideas. However, it was only under the vigorous dictatorship of its temporary rulers that Venezuela succeeded in attaining to conditions of prosperity. After interminable struggles, the country enjoyed two comparatively prolonged periods of well-being. The first began in 1875 under the rule of Guzman Blanco. He was the man who delivered himself on his deathbed of a remark that has since become famous. When his confessor adjured him to forgive his enemies, he said, 'I can't, I've killed them all'.

After him came the prodigious Castro, who, with his ignorance and vainglorious pretentiousness, gave umbrage to the great European powers and drew upon himself naval demonstrations by Germany and England. And then, in 1913, began the presidency of Juan Vicente Gomez. To-day Juan Vicente Gomez is still in power. He has reorganized the finances, the army and the civil service, and by his firmness, given peace to his country. The wisdom and caution of his rule have resulted in the extinction of all internal debts. The natural resources of Venezuela suffice to provide for the needs of the budget and the Venezuelans are, together with the citizens of

Monaco, the only inhabitants of a modern state who enjoy immunity from taxation. It is true that petrol exploitation accounts for a good deal of this. The Venezuelan government is unique. It is a dictatorship run on heavy oil.

ECUADOR

LIKE Venezuela, Ecuador separated from the Republic of Colombia in 1831. Undisturbed by Federalist conflicts, it had suffered from nothing more serious than quarrels between conservatives and democrats. As in most of the other countries of South America, these internal dissensions have been virtually continuous, only being interrupted by the ephemeral domination of some transient dictator. The first of these was Juan Flores, the companion of Bolivar and Rocafuerte, who proved himself a capable administrator, put the finances in order, organized popular education, created a civil and a penal code and renewed friendly relations with Spain. Flores subsequently returned to power, was overthrown, made war on the new government and finally paved the way to the Presidency for his son-in-law, Gabriel Gorcia Moreno, who was born in 1841.

Moreno was an educated and fairly broad-minded man and Ecuador prospered under his dictatorship. To him was due the construction of roads, ports, hospitals and schools. Unfortunately these works cost a great deal of money and the dictator was obliged to introduce the compulsory employment of paper money which considerably diminished his popularity. It soon became known that in order to cope with the financial crisis, Moreno had formally asked protection of France and afterwards of Spain. His Concordat with Rome, which was highly advantageous to the Church, completed his undoing. External disputes with Colombia and Peru dealt an additional blow to his reputation. Nevertheless, with the aid of the clergy, Moreno maintained himself in power for several years, until, in 1874, he fell a victim to an assassin's dagger. Though there is great divergency of opinion regarding him, there is no denying that Ecuador enjoyed a period of unexampled prosperity under his rule. He was violent and unscrupulous and may possibly have lacked that jealous love for his country which seems to have been the rule. But he was a daring administrator, and his audacity paid, inasmuch as, at his death, the country's finances were flourishing. In private life he was a man whose sincere and lively faith was worthy of all respect. Without the favouring influence of the clergy, who developed his missions and helped to Christianize the Indians, he would never have been able to maintain his position. Possibly, however, he might have obtained a more favourable verdict from republican historians, who regard him with deep resentment for having brought back to this land of freedom those very monastic orders by whom, in days gone by, it had been enslaved, or, in other words, civilized.

BOLIVIA

BOLIVIA, formerly known as Upper Peru, had assumed its name as a mark of its admiration for the Liberator, who received the title of Protector and President. General Sucre, who had been in command of the army of independence, gave his name to the capital of Chuquisaca. It was Bolivar who drew up the Constitution, which goes by the name of the Bolivian Code, and which furnishes the principal written repository of his political ideas.

An elaborately graduated register of electors set forth the names of the persons entitled to vote. They elected the members of the three Chambers: The Tribunes, the Senate and the Censors, these latter being guardians of the Constitution and umpires between the other two. As to the executive power, that was to be in the hands of a Life-President, assisted by a Vice-President nominated by the President and his legal successor. The exercise of these functions was temporarily conferred by Bolivar on General Sucre. But all this was too good to last.

We have seen that Bolivia lost no time in severing relations with its liberator and in repudiating his constitution. It was General Santa-Cruz who provided it with a new one, before allowing his country to enter upon disastrous wars with the neighbouring States, especially with Peru.

There followed a period of confusion and unheavals of wearisome monotony. One after another, victorious generals would seize the reins of government and hold them for six months or possibly a year and then promptly give place to the very generals they had so recently vanquished. In the swift procession of governments and parties, of men and ideas, the national consciousness seems to grow non-existent. The army is the only force that counts, the army and the leader in command of it.

Of all the States of South America, Bolivia is the one for which Bolivar seems to have had a particular regard. He framed another Constitution for it which, though unquestionably susceptible of improvement, stressed the paramount importance of order, strong government and continuity; three virtues which Bolivia seems to have set itself perseveringly to disown.

THE ARGENTINE REPUBLIC

AFTER the quarrels between the federalists and the nationalists which were the immediate sequel of the declaration of independence, the Argentine Republic, in its turn, quickly made acquaintance with the rule of a *candillo*, backed by a band of *gauchos* whom he had rallied to his support in the plains. They were the kind of men who would stick at nothing. The *candillo* in question was the celebrated Don Juan Manuel Ortiz de Rosas.

He was the most eccentric dictator that Latin America ever produced. It by no means followed that he was the mildest.

When, in 1828, he began to be talked about, he was a man of thirty-five. Hitherto his whole life had been spent among the cowboys on the family estates. As far back as 1820, he had led his men to the support of the nationalists. In 1827, he had called them up on behalf of the federalists. In 1829, he was appointed governor and captain-general of Buenos Aires. 'You have called me to govern according to my lights and the dictates of my conscience. I will do so. My convictions shall be my guide. To make them prevail shall be my duty.'

It was rather a stern dictatorship. He began by making war on the nationalists, a war which stands out as ruthless even in a land where ruthlessness was the rule. But he also put an end to the raids of the Indian tribesmen of the southern pampas, and the popularity of

Rosas, industriously fanned by a cleverly manipulated and strictly censored press, assumed considerable proportions among the masses.

He prevailed on the Chamber to entrust him with plenary powers to act as he thought best in the public interest, a measure which was confirmed by a plebiscite. Every five years Rosas pleaded with the Chamber to let him retire, and every five years the Chamber decreed him fresh honours. He remained in power until 1852.

The *gauchos* nicknamed him the Washington of the South, though he had little in common with his alleged prototype. But he was at all events a man of lively intelligence and immense capacity for hard work. Every department of the public service was under his control, army, police, finance, press, civil service, diplomacy. The strictest discipline was maintained about his person and the mass executions ordered by him have long been a standing reproach against him in the eyes of his opponents. Entirely without scruple, he displayed an ingenuity not far short of genius in inventing fresh devices to add gruesomeness and horror to his acts of terrorism. In Buenos Aires one morning, hawkers were going about shouting, 'Peaches, fine peaches!' When people went up to them to look in their baskets, they were aghast to find the bleeding heads of the rebels who had been condemned to death the previous day.

Rosas was overthrown by an insurrection in the provinces, in which Brazil had a finger. After a brief but desperate struggle, he escaped on board a British vessel and sought refuge with his daughter in Ireland. Although he had always boasted that he was a federalist, he had had scant regard for the claims of the provinces. Henceforth Buenos Aires played the predominant role in Argentine policy, and it was Rosas who contributed not a little to make that great port what it afterwards became. But his tyranny, for it was nothing less, and his merciless acts of repression had taken the heart out of his subordinates. The stranger stepped in, and people forgot the debt they owed him.

Thereafter, passing from one civil war to another, Argentina shared the customary fate of the South American nations, despite her outstanding commercial prosperity. In other words, *candillos*, more or less transitory, followed one another in swift succession, and the country enjoyed no real peace save when the government possessed some degree of stability. Thus, for thirty years, it was General Julian Roca who was the real director of national policy. He so far adopted Bolivar's methods as to appoint his own successor, and saw to it that the official candidate always won. The Argentinians called this 'presidential posterity'. And thus it was that, even when Roca was not himself in power, he (like Nunez in Colombia) was the actual ruler of the country, the power behind the throne.

URUGUAY AND PARAGUAY

URUGUAY, the smallest of the South American States, was no exception to the common rule. Manuel Oribe, in 1835, and subsequently Pereira, or Barnardo Berro, were true dictators, as also were Flores and Elluari after them. Unhappily for the country, none of them was strong enough to maintain order for any length of time, in face of warring factions and conflicts with foreign powers.

To begin with, Paraguay looked like being an exception. Right down to 1865, this ancient and very extraordinary creation of the Jesuits lived on in profound peace, totally indifferent to the political passions by which other nations were torn and distracted. It was governed, it must be confessed, by a strange creature, one Francia, who, in 1814, had been elected its supreme and perpetual dictator.

Francia's dearest aim seems to have been to isolate Paraguay from the rest of the world. Any traveller who set foot within its borders was flung into prison. There was once a botanist who spent ten long years in a dungeon there.

Francia was a man fairly well on in years (he was then fifty-nine). He was highly educated and had once had serious thoughts of entering the priesthood. Free with his own money, but very careful of the State's, he had small love for the Church, to which he had once so nearly belonged. Nevertheless, it was from the Church that he borrowed the isolation policy which had been so dear to the Jesuits.

Whatever may be said about him, he did succeed in maintaining peace and order, a sufficiently rare achievement on this continent to call for admiration. He gave a great impetus to the development of industry and organized for the benefit of the State a system of trade and barter in respect of the agricultural produce of the country. Inasmuch, however, as total isolation was scarcely compatible with commerce, it was not long before he relaxed some of the severity of his earlier regulations. Nevertheless, he still retained the right to supervise the terms of every transaction, public or private. It was a somewhat strange economic arrangement.

Francia cut roads, improved the defences of the towns, founded a military port, organized the army and surrounded himself with a powerful bodyguard, for he went in fear of his life. He lived with his barber, like the Louis XI of the popular history books, together with four slaves. At seventy years of age he married a young French woman.

Habitually attired in a uniform coat lavishly adorned with gold lace and cut, as he was pleased to think, like Bonaparte's, the old man governed Paraguay with a rule so absolute that very few countries can show anything resembling it. Living in perpetual dread of some fresh conspiracy, he gave orders that, whenever he passed along the streets, people should lie down with their faces to the ground. A veritable atmosphere of terror surrounded him. He died on the 20th September, 1840, at the age of eighty-three, after nearly knocking his doctor senseless. So ended this unusual personage, who remains a perpetual enigma in the history of dictatorships.

He was succeeded, first by his nephew, Antonio Lopez, and then by the latter's son, Solano Lopez, who endeavoured to break away from Francia's policy and opened up relations between Paraguay and other American and European countries. Unluckily, later on, an outbreak of war destroyed the power of this strange dynasty and involved the country in a disaster from which it took a long time to recover.

PERU

In 1826, Peru had received a similar Constitution to that of its neighbour, Bolivia, and like Bolivia, it was soon to discard it. Its earlier annals are full of the struggles between its various dictators, Gamarra, Lafuente, Vivanco. These dictators did not work alone. They had intrepid wives, half-Indian amazons, who, when their husbands' powers began to flag, put themselves at the head of the troops and, with plumes streaming out behind them in the wind, went forth to conquer cities. Doña Cypriano Vivanco set all hearts on fire. Her fame was sung by all the bards. She presided at the bull-fights. The brief supremacy of Vivanco was a dictatorship of love-making.

He made the unfortunate mistake of exiling a certain general, the son of an Indian wanderer who, like Paez, had an armed following. This man, after an interlude by the prefect Elias, promptly possessed himself of the supreme power. He was Ramon Castilla, a man of great energy, forthright in his ideas and a strong believer in authority. Like Bolivar and Paez, he quickly realized the need for a strong government. From 1844 to 1862, he directed the national policy, strengthened the foundations of peace, befriended education and created a fleet. He gave the slaves their freedom, and worked for the emancipation and education of the native Indians. He was the first to see commercial possibilities in the systematic exploitation of guano.

Castilla had adopted as his own the motto of Louis XIV, '*L'Etat, c'est moi*'. When he deemed that the time had come to retire, he himself selected his successor, in the Bolivarian manner. After him, a succession of moderately wise presidents maintained order amid grave difficulties, of which a war with Spain was one. Castilla died in 1867, after attempting to provoke a rising against General Prado.

In 1872, Manuel Prado assumed the reins of government and devoted himself with energy to the task of reforming the army. He also addressed himself to the business of organizing the municipal services, suppressing supernumerary officials, and, like all dictators, setting the country's financial house in order. The finances of Peru were in a very shaky condition and guano was no longer a sufficient source of income. The State took over the saltpetre monopoly and so increased the yield from guano that it presently furnished three-quarters of the national income. Despite the war with Chile, which was to prove so arduous a struggle, it is unquestionably to Castillo and Prado that Peru owes its prosperity.

CHILE

CHILE, after a few initial crises, has enjoyed a comparatively peaceful existence. It is a sort of aristocratic republic, in which the majority of the population, as in the days of the Spanish domination, live the lives of farmers or tillers of the soil, and keep up their patriarchal customs. For this reason Chile has often been held up as an example to other American nations. One of the founders of the State, San Martin, a friend of Bolivar's, and a president — though not for long — lost no time in introducing the ideas and examples of the illustrious Liberator.

But the man who had most influence over Chile's destinies, though his appearance was a brief one, was Portales. It was he who inspired the charter of 1833, and worked so hard to secure the re-election of Soreto, the first president. He was soon to disappear and in tragic fashion, yet, simple and comparatively uneducated as he was, he did a great deal for his country. The reform of the clergy, of the Courts of Justice, the creation of a National Guard, the organization of the police, and above all the restoration of confidence — these were Portales' most conspicuous titles to the gratitude of his country. Like Moreno in Ecuador and Castilla in Peru, Portales, for one brief space, was the soul of his country. Towards the close of the century, President George Montt, a liberal and an anti-clerical, endeavoured to rally the patriots around him, and to some extent succeeded. But he was not so successful as Portales.

However, these dictators, who passed across the scene so swiftly, though great men in their own land, are scarcely known outside it, unless it be to stamp-collectors to whom their features are familiar.

BRAZIL

THE most extensive of the South American States, Brazil, has had a destiny peculiar to itself. It was once a Portuguese colony, and Portuguese is still the official language there. In 1805, fleeing before the French army, the Royal Court of Portugal came to crave hospitality of its opulent colony in the New World. In 1815, Brazil was promoted to the rank of a kingdom. In 1817, at Pernambuco, the curé Ribeiro, a diligent student of Condorcet, 'the breath of whose life was freedom', fomented an insurrection and proclaimed a republic. Curé Ribeiro's head was seen soon after in the streets of Pernambuco on the end of a pike, but still John VI, Emperor and King of Brazil and Portugal, did not feel easy in his mind. Lisbon wanted him back, and his son Don Pedro urged him to be accommodating. In 1821, John VI embarked for Portugal, leaving behind him his twenty-two-year-old son, as regent. In 1822, the cleavage between Europe and America became an accomplished fact, and Don Pedro was proclaimed as constitutional Emperor of Brazil.

Thus Brazil was the solitary American State to possess, for any length of time, a settled dynasty. For their boldness and intelligence, the princes of the House of Braganza, transplanted to a country not their own, well merited the title of dictators and kings. Don Pedro wrote to his father that the only way to preserve Brazil to his line, was to convert it into an independent monarchy,

Great Britain urged John VI to accept the inevitable, and so the separation took place.

We should say in the political jargon of these days, that Pedro was more or less a partisan of the Left. He even went so far as to proclaim himself Grand Master of the Freemasons, but as soon as he was sure of his position, he ordered the Masonic lodges to be suppressed and pronounced the dissolution of the first Constituent Assembly. While he was coping with partial risings and the difficulties which England had put in his way, his father John VI died, and in 1825 he inherited the crown of Portugal. This he resigned in favour of his daughter, Doña Maria, a proceeding which gave rise to not a few dissensions in Europe in which both France and England thought it their business to interfere. In 1831, following an enactment restricting the freedom of the press, the capital rose in revolt and Don Pedro was compelled to abdicate in favour of his son, a child of six. He took the strange step of appointing as the lad's guardian, the leader of the democratic party, then an exile in Bordeaux.

In 1841, the young Emperor Pedro II, by that time fifteen years of age, was crowned with every circumstance of solemnity. Shortly afterwards he began to rule in earnest. Pedro II was an Emperor with up-to-date ideas, very intelligent, and very adroit and, by skilfully steering the ship of state in and out among the reefs of the rival parties he contrived to preserve both his crown and public order. He respected the freedom of the press, knowing full well how important it was to have the newspapers on his side, and he maintained at least the outward semblance of a parliamentary régime. People were under the impression that he reigned but did not rule. For all that, he exerted a considerable influence on the nation. A war against Rosas, and another with Paraguay, failed to mar the general tranquillity of his long reign. With conspicuous address, he settled the various religious crises that arose, always a source of danger, and in 1862 abolished the traffic in slaves that still existed at that time. In 1871, the sons of slaves were granted their freedom, though it was not until 1888 that slavery was completely done away with.

It was Pedro II who gave particular encouragement to foreign immigration. The Germans especially poured in large numbers into the country and for a time this wholesale invasion gave rise to considerable uneasiness. A section of the press gave utterance to the foreboding that it might one day threaten a disruption.

Although, when Pedro II's reign came to an end, Brazil had shouldered a portion of the Portuguese national debt, the finances of the country were in a flourishing condition. Expenditure was inconsiderable, the army and navy were in a satisfactory state and the budget showed a surplus. Unfortunately, in 1889, the Emperor who had become blind, was playing but an insignificant part in public affairs. He was very popular, but his officers, having taken counsel together in the military academies, engineered a kind of headquarters' revolution with the object of removing him from power. The intellectuals who, under the influence of Benjamin Constant, had become converts to a sort of hotch-potch of liberalism and positivism, joined forces with the officers. At the end of 1889, the Republic was proclaimed and the imperial family were sent into exile. Floriano Peixoto's sanguinary dictatorship made people wish they had got them back again. However, it lasted no great while, and, after it, Brazil made acquaintance with parliamentary rule in a variety of phases.

Latin America, of whose history we have just given all too brief a sketch, is that part of the world in whose annals we may most clearly discern the dangers of anarchy. None of its States, save Brazil, boasts a royal dynasty. None possesses a genuine aristocracy. In order to live, to keep clear of the terrible tyranny exercised by party over party, and to avoid strife between the divers social and racial elements that compose the population of these countries, one means and one alone presents itself, and that is dictatorship. Without a dictatorship, there is no alternative but anarchy and civil war.

The profoundest intellect of South America, Simon Bolivar, when all around him people were still proclaiming their belief in the doctrines of the eighteenth century, when the disciples of Rousseau held, with their master, 'that you make a people as you make a lock' and that 'societies in the hands of the legislator are as clay in the hands of the potter', Simon Bolivar maintained that constitutions should be adapted to the character of the peoples for whom they were intended.

The only dictatorships which have succeeded in Latin America are those which have had the means to persist, which have had driving power behind them and which have shown themselves at once beneficent and strong. And they have been almost always of popular origin. Men like Paez, Rosas or Castilla were all sons of the prairie.

They were swift to show a capacity for rule that was little hampered by moral preoccupations. Notwithstanding their excesses, it was due to them that nations a prey to all the restless agitations of untutored youth were able to take shape and to endure. The romantic story of the worst of them contains passages that send a thrill to the heart. They shepherded their people as they did their flocks and herds; they broke them in, as they broke in their horses.

Here is another piece of advice to countries that would fain avoid the hardships of emergency governments. Never put yourselves in the position of being unable to do without them.

THE PRESENT DAY

THE BOLSHEVIK DICTATORS
ANTECEDENTS AND PRELIMINARIES
OF THE RUSSIAN REVOLUTION

RUSSIA, throughout the nineteenth century, had been the classic ground of terrorism. One of its most beneficent rulers, Alexander II, the Imperial liberator, had died a violent death! Western Europe had no very clear idea of what these revolutionaries were, and lumped them all together indiscriminately, under one name — 'nihilists'. What was undeniable about them, however, was their violence and their tenacity.

The police and the law, brutal and often arbitrary and stupid in their operations, seldom distinguished between leaders and led. They sometimes hanged college lads of sixteen and sent dangerous agitators like Vladimir Ilitch Oulianov, the future Lenin, to spend a few years of pleasant exile in Siberia.

The *intelligentsia*, like most Russian men of letters of those days, were nearly all pledged to the anti-Tzarist cause. As far back as 1896 the Militant Union, founded by Lenin, had got together some hundred public speakers all of them 'intellectuals'.

Thanks to the fanaticism of these fighting leaders, expressed in the motto 'All or Nothing', and thanks to the all-important services they rendered as spies, extremist views and opinions went on steadily gaining ground in spite of the censorship and of every possible form of repression. Meanwhile countless assassinations,

railway sabotage, bank hold-ups and strikes with violence, encouraged under any and every pretext, familiar-
ized supporters of the movement with danger, accustomed
them to direct action and created an appropriately revolutionary background and tradition.

This propaganda was naturally addressed, in the first
place, to the new proletariat of St. Petersburg and of
industrial centres like Baku, and loyalty to the throne,
which, in the early stages, was professed by the working-
men in stating their grievances could not hold its own
for very long against the vigorous activities of the
Militant Union.

The adhesion of the Russian Socialists to the orthodox
Marxist profession of faith was an accomplished fact as
far back as 1897. Nihilism, among the most notable of
whose crimes were those of the famous 'Executive Committee', was henceforth a thing of the past, but its deeds
of violence had tempered and trained the spirits of the
Bolsheviks of the morrow.

In 1903, a congress which opened in Brussels and was
afterwards transferred to London constituted the Social
Democratic Federation of Russian Working Men. Out
of its fifty-eight delegates, only four were manual workers.

At their meetings, these intellectuals, from the very
outset, spent all their energies in arguments and discussions rudely interrupted by the brutal demands and
frigidly deliberate calumnies hurled at them by Lenin,
the leader of these debates, who had made up his mind
to become the incarnate symbol of the party and to
banish the waverers and circumlocutionists from its
ranks.

A few months later the party definitely split into minimists or mensheviks and maximists or bolsheviks, with Lenin at their head. He was then just thirty-three.

The Russo-Japanese war of 1904-1905 was soon to provide the revolutionaries with an opportunity to make their power felt.

On the 22nd January, 1905, two hundred thousand workmen, under the leadership of the monk Gapone, the bearer of a petition, marched in procession, but without arms, to the Winter Palace. They were greeted with a hurricane of lead and some hundreds of them were shot dead.

That was the 'Red Sunday' that kindled the flame of widespread insurrection. The disasters of Port Arthur, Mukden and Tsushima, the terrible death roll at the front, the food shortage at home, made the government unpopular even with the middle classes, who had been possessed by a spirit of defeatism from the very commencement of the war. The people rose as one man in the four corners of the Empire. The long sequence of red outrages still went on. The Grand-Duke Serge, the Tsar's uncle, was murdered. At Moscow there were simultaneous strikes involving some millions of workers, street fighting went on in the various industrial centres, incendiarism and looting were rife throughout the country. 1905 for the Empire was a year of downright civil war. In Poland and Armenia, the disturbances took the form of national separatist movements. There was a naval mutiny at Sebastopol and Cronstadt.

In October, Lenin secretly recrossed the frontier.

The disorders which had extended to the whole of Russia were now reaching their height.

Hiding in Moscow, Lenin set to work to organize a revolution. As he had no use for the undisciplined *levée en masse*, he elaborated a system of insurrection on military lines. It was to be led by little groups of professional revolutionaries with certain definite objectives. Under their skilled leadership, less than two thousand workers kept General Doubasov's whole army, ten times their number, at bay for nine days. At last they had to surrender to mere weight of numbers.

While the mutterings of revolt were still audible from the Black Sea to the White, Lenin, deeming that this round of the fight had been lost, crossed the Finnish frontier and proceeded to plot his revenge in exile, heedless of the murmurs that taxed him with deserting the cause.

These early results put new heart into the revolutionary *emigrés*, and they did not slacken their activities. The Bolshevik Party was definitely founded in 1912, with a Central Committee consisting of seven members.

For seven whole years, now in Paris, now in Zurich, Lenin, a little, well-behaved, modest, black-coated clerk, betook himself day by day to the public libraries to read up the German philosophers and more especially the German strategists, and worked on with confident tenacity at forging the weapons of revolution. Setting systematically to work, he purged the party of the opportunists, the word-spinners, the *aventuristes* (like Trotsky, be it whispered), and of all doctrinaires suspected of cherishing democratic illusions. To such as would have it that salvation lay in maintaining a united socialist front, he answered, in the words of Karl Marx, that 'insurrection is an art' and that what he wanted was a band of trained revolutionaries. To those who favoured a revolution by the democratic method, he retorted that 'a revolution is incontestably the most authoritative thing there is'. And he mentally selected the men, who, after the revolution had been carried out, would be indispensable in coping with the forces of counter-revolution. He emphasized the ineluctable necessity for a dictator to crush the resistance of the bourgeoisie, to terrorize reactionaries and to uphold the authority of the people in arms. 'Such a dictatorship must be a power based directly on force.' He did not hesitate to say 'the new régime could only be kept in existence by the most sanguinary of tyrannies'. All this argumentative cut-and-thrust though it seemed unintelligible to the fighters in far-off Russia, gained Lenin some of his most fanatical supporters, lent vigour to his teaching, enabled him to define his aims, and imparted a sharper edge to his inflexible determination.

The tocsin of 1914 drowned the muttered storm of the strikes which had broken out again more fiercely than ever. The Russian mobilization was carried out in good order. Under the influence of Jules Guesde, the social-democrats, mensheviks and revolutionary socialists rallied, almost unanimously, to the *union sacrée*, resolved to repel the forces of German militarism.

Lenin chaffed them brutally: all he could see in the war was 'a quarrel between slave-drivers wrangling about their human cattle'. And he asserted that the only possible policy for the proletariat to pursue was to oppose all national defence without discrimination. Moreover he was confident that this war meant revolution.

His words were soon justified by events. The internal disintegration of the Empire was accelerated by defeatism. Treason, spying and extortion were rife on every hand. The *morale* of the troops and of the population grew feebler month by month. The Duma was not to be trusted. The Tsar, though full of good intentions, was deserted and powerless. The majority of the aristocracy and the upper middle classes had abandoned him. Everyone was plotting for his own ends: some wanted a regency, others a republic.

On the 6th March it was 43 degrees below freezing point at St. Petersburg. All the hot water pipes had burst, trains were at a standstill. No corn was coming into the city. Nevertheless, in socialist circles there was never less idea of a revolution. On the morning of the 8th March, a certain Kerensky, a social-revolutionary deputy, asserted that a rising was impossible at the moment.

Nevertheless, at noon it broke out without the slightest warning. The workmen downed tools and went and looted the bakers' shops. On the 9th, all the suburbs followed suit. The garrison consisted of a hundred thousand men. But the Cossacks fired on the police, instead of charging the mob. Most of the regiments started fraternizing with the demonstrators. In a hundred hours, the Tzarist regime was overthrown by an irresistible onslaught. On the 11th, Nicholas II abdicated at his Army Headquarters. The grand-dukes hoisted the red flag above their palaces. The Imperial Guard went over to the rebels. The revolution was accomplished and it had not cost five hundred lives.

The proletarians had risen of their own accord. Their lack of leadership immediately made itself felt. The Duma slavishly formed a provisional government, with Kerensky as prime minister. Side by side with it, a Soviet was constituted, consisting of working men and soldiers, mensheviks for the most part. These two mutually antagonistic organizations undertook to share the government and from the 14th March there was an open breach between them. The Provisional Government decided unanimously to continue the war. The Soviet issued a peace manifesto to all the nations of the world.

The ensuing months saw things going from bad to worse. The war went on, in virtue of the principle that it was the duty of a democracy to resist German Im- perialism. The economic crisis became more acute. The Provisional Government vacillated, temporized, and postponed for week after week the summoning of that Constituent Assembly which everyone hoped would save the situation. The Soviet was looking for 'a *via media* between demagogy and reaction'. The long awaited agrarian laws did not materialize. Lenin was in Switzer- land when he heard the tidings from St. Petersburg. How was he going to get back to Russia? He immediately set to work to examine the various possibilities. The German Headquarters Staff, which realized what an admirable ally they would have in this hungry doctrinaire with his thirty odd determined disciples about him, granted him a free passage through German territory — but it was in a sealed carriage. The party reached St. Petersburg on the 3rd April, and were greeted with enthusiasm by the Bolshevik faction.

In his first speech, Lenin demanded that plenary powers should be given to workmen's Soviets instead of to a parliamentary republic. He called for the suppression of the police and the civil service; the abolition of the Provisional Government which he said was oligarchical, and demanded that the Russian troops should fraternize with the Germans at the front. These plans filled the Bolsheviks with consternation and provoked the irony of the social-democrats, whose newspapers took the view that Lenin talked too much nonsense to be dangerous.

In the middle of July, rioting among the workers, soldiers and sailors flared up anew at St. Petersburg and Cronstadt. For their slogan, the rioters adopted the Lenin formula 'All power to the Soviets'. Kerensky, in a panic, recalled some generals from the front with sixty thousand men to smash the movement. He succeeded. It was generally supposed that he would bring off a counter-revolution. The moderates breathed again. Lenin was charged with high treason, and again had to cross the frontier. He left for Finland disguised as a chauffeur and wearing a ginger wig. But the fugitive took with him the certainty that his triumph would not be long delayed.

Alas, the weeks went by and Kerensky became more and more deeply involved in the mire of futile verbiage, trying to frighten the generals with the revolutionaries, and the revolutionaries with the generals.

It was not long before he committed an irretrievable mistake. General Kornilov, sick of his endless prevarications, marched on St. Petersburg. Kerensky, at his wits' end, flung open the prisons, let out the Bolshevik sailors and soldiers he had arrested in July, and sent them off to engage the General. Kornilov surrendered, as it turned out, without striking a blow. But Kerensky was henceforth suspect in the eyes of the social-democrats and the Bolsheviks were at large again.

From this point onwards, Lenin, safe in his retreat, worked with feverish energy to precipitate a decision. Early in October, his cranium still adorned with the ginger wig, he made his way back into Russia and hid himself in a suburb of the capital.

The provisional government was in a state of complete deliquescence. Its Right Wing and its Left Wing had alike deserted it. The army took French leave. At the front it was thought that peace might be proclaimed any day. It was calculated that there were two million deserters scattered about the country. Disorder was at its height in St. Petersburg. The streets were thronged day and night by a solid mass of humanity, and meetings took place one after another in endless succession.

Meantime Kerensky, unlucky as usual in his prophecies, stood up like a hero and said 'There's only one thing I want. Let the Bolsheviks come. I will down them. Russia is with us to a man. Fear nothing.' Incapable of ordering the arrest of the military commission which was working with frenzied haste at the Smolny Institute, he told off twenty thousand men on whom he could rely to guard the public buildings. But Trotsky, with whom Lenin had become reconciled, Trotsky who was the real tactician of the Bolshevik army, did not care a straw about public buildings. What could he do with them? No; he knew a trick worth two of that. He resolved to go for the technical nerve-centres of the State: telegraph, telephone, general post office, electric generating station, railways. For the past ten days he had been having plans drawn of these places by gangs of bolsheviks disguised as workmen. Trotsky did not favour a general strike (the trades unions were timid and divided). Besides there was no need of one. The continual rioting in the streets was enough to paralyse the life of the place. He had hardly more than a thousand men at his command, but they were split up into squads, each with its own defined sector and objective. They knew exactly where they were to go and what they were to do. 'To get control of a modern State, you want a body of stormtroops and technicians, gangs of armed men with engineers to tell them what to do.'

On the 24th October, the date selected by the Soviet Congress, Trotsky gave orders for the blow to be struck. The Red Guards gained possession of the bridges and telegraph stations without any difficulty. Sailors seized the railway stations, the gasworks, and the central electric generating station. Armoured cars kept the communications between the different gangs intact. At six o'clock in the evening, the provisional government, now entirely cut off from the rest of the country, took refuge in the Winter Palace. The whole city was out of doors. No one realized that the Bolsheviks were virtually masters of the situation, not even Lenin himself. Lenin was fidgety and wanted things to move faster. He was afraid things would be held up, he got flustered. But on the 25th, Trotsky's troops, backed by the guns of the cruiser *Aurora*, stormed the Winter Palace. Kerensky fled for his life. Lenin then divested himself of his ginger wig and appeared before the Soviet Congress, who cheered him to the echo, and proclaimed the fall of the provisional government.

LENIN, DICTATOR

THE same anarchical conditions which had enabled Lenin to put himself in power, proved a serious obstacle to the establishment and development of the revolutionary régime.

The Bolshevik programme, minutely elaborated in advance, was a multifarious one. It comprised the immediate convocation of a Constituent Assembly; the abolition of capital punishment; the recognition of the independence of the several nationalities that had been included within the framework of the late Empire; distribution of land among the peasants; abolition of the police force, of the army and of government officialdom; suppression of privileges; equal pay for all; peaceful rivalry of the various political parties under the aegis of the Soviets.

Not one item of this programme of abstractions was found to be practicable.

The Bolsheviks for the most part had made up their minds that the triumph of their party, the defection of the Russian Army and the fraternization of their soldiers with the enemy would have a decisive effect on all the belligerents; that, following their example, everyone would agree to a peace without victors or vanquished, what time the proletariats of the entire world would be preparing for the final conflict of the classes.

But the terrible conditions laid down by the Germans soon disillusioned them. The negotiations were deliberately dragged out. Many, like Trotsky, said it were better for the revolutionary forces to make war than to sign a disgraceful peace with the Prussian feudatories. But an ultimatum from Berlin compelled them to face the facts. There was no making war with an army that had already been undermined by Marxist propaganda. If the Germans did not get what they demanded, they would invade the whole country and then what would happen to the revolution? Stifling the complaints of his colleagues — most of them were expressing their discontent — Lenin made it clear to them that they had no choice in the matter. No better terms he said were to be had, and he for his part would be willing to accept conditions a hundred times more degrading, because there was no other way of keeping the revolution in being.

The result was the treaty of Brest-Litovsk.

The meeting of the Constituent Assembly 'representing the sweated working classes' was, in the domain of ideas, another reverse. The Bolsheviks only got a quarter of the votes. The peasantry plumped for the socialist revolutionaries without being capable of distinguishing Right from Left. The Constituent was dissolved by a decree of Lenin's the day after it had held its first meeting. A 'red' sailor marched into the Chamber, went up to the President's chair, clapped a hand on his shoulder and showed him the door. It was all over with the Democratic Republic.

Freedom of the press for the other socialist parties, which had been adopted on principle as a measure of conciliation, was found untenable as soon as the other papers began their attacks, Gorki's paper in particular, which described Bolshevism as 'a national calamity'. Still less was there any chance for that 'friendly party rivalry'.

As and when these difficulties made their appearance, Lenin dropped one item of his programme after another in favour of one single aim: the keeping of the Bolsheviks in power. As he put it, 240,000 Bolsheviks could easily do the work which the 130,000 landed proprietors, who had previously directed the destinies of Russia, had done before them.

Whatever may have been left of the initial reform scheme soon disappeared amid the twofold crisis that now fell on the country; the peasant revolt and the civil war.

One of the first things the dictator saw to was the promulgation of the agrarian law. It abolished the great landholdings, but failed to form any genuinely collective system of territorial exploitation. The peasants shared the usufruct of the lands. Rosa Luxemburg very justly observed that in designing, by this means, to win over the peasants, the revolutionary leaders were out in their reckoning. Such a splitting up of the soil mitigated against the tendency to economic centralization implicit in the new form of government. 'The measure was not only non-socialist, but it barred the road that led to socialism.' What was created was not socialistic property, but a property split up into parcels, the method of whose cultivation necessarily registered a technical decline compared with that of the great estates. The parcelling out of the land, which was necessarily arbitrary, had the inevitable effect of intensifying the old inequality in favour of the *Kulaks* or well-to-do peasants. In point of fact the land-distribution decrees did not recognize the *status quo*, seeing that ever since October the peasants had shared out the land on their own initiative.

But the situation in Russia grew more and more tragic and this mutual allocation of the soil was soon to prove an illusion. The armistice put an end to the struggle on the various fronts, but civil war was spreading ruin and devastation through what yesterday had been the Russian Empire.

From the end of 1918, to the autumn of the year following, the red armies had a rough handling on the Volga, at Perm, on the Eastern front. General Ioudenitch pushed them back northwards to the very gates of St. Petersburg.

During this chaotic period, Russia, as in all her troublous times, experienced the horrors of famine. Lenin paid no heed to that. He was convinced that a worldwide revolution was bound to come. He felt that what Bolshevism had to do at all costs was to hold on. He set every wheel turning to procure this great consummation, and instituted 'war communism'.

The first consequence of this new communism was the forcible commandeering of farm produce from the peasants who, suddenly as they had become landowners, now found themselves as suddenly reduced to beggary. These brutal exactions were carried out under the control of the agricultural soviets. They roused the fury of the *moujiks* who took to hiding their cereals. They gave

rise to appalling persecutions and massacres. A cruel
guerilla war, more sanguinary even than the civil war,
accounted for nearly a million victims among the
peasants alone.

Furthermore, the struggle involved the militarization
of the Bolshevik party. Capital punishment was, we
need not add, also reinstated in the army as well as
among the civil population, so were decorations, which
had likewise been abolished. The extraordinary commission or Cheka, which saw to the carrying out of
martial law, was a hundred times more rigorous and
bloodthirsty than the corresponding Tzarist organizations.

As for the principle of nationality, that was con-
spicuously flouted in Georgia, where an experiment in
running an independent and federal republic was attempted. It was broken up by the Reds. Trotsky
brushed aside the famous principle by the simple question he put to the Georgian mensheviks. 'Does the right
of self-determination among nations mean that they have
the right to injure their neighbours with impunity?'

By means of this remorseless tyranny, the most
murderous that any nation has ever undergone, Lenin
made sure of his position as dictator. The Soviets now
counted for no more than trained flunkeys, voting, as
they were told to vote, for any measure that was considered necessary. The Cheka continued to function
and spread its network over the whole country. The
trade unions were kept well in hand, like the Soviets.
The various departments of State had been monopolized
by the Bolsheviks and were but obsequious tributaries

of the two supreme bodies: the *Politbureau* (political bureau) and the *Orgbureau* (organization bureau) composed of only five members, from whom all decisions of importance proceeded. 'A regular oligarchy,' Lenin cynically remarked.

Naturally there was henceforth no room for any party other than the Bolshevik, and the press was completely muzzled.

However, after the horrors of the worst of civil wars, a war in which the Bolsheviks applied the systematic cruelty advocated by Lenin and Trotsky, Russia encountered a fate perhaps more tragic still.

The extreme difficulty of food-commandeering in regions where ruin or rioting reigned supreme, the disorganization of the transport services which were always very uncertain, brought famine again to the greater part of the country, and, singularly enough, to the great centres of population.

The greater part of the controlling class had been murdered, or had fled the country, so that industry had no one to direct it. The yield of the factories taken over by the state fell to less than twenty per cent of the pre-war output. The process of socializing degenerated from systematic sabotage to wanton destruction. 'Already,' Lenin confessed, 'we have confiscated, nationalized, smashed and demolished more than we can put on record.'

Bolshevism, meandering off after its initial success, announced that money was going to be done away with. This was the last word in progress. It had already been admitted in principle that the State should provide for all the requirements of its workers. All it succeeded in doing was to eke out miserable rations which grew ever more scanty as the months went by. In thickly populated towns it was impossible to procure such bare necessities as clothes, salt, sugar, coal, wood, etc.

Repeated reverses of this kind at length made it clear to Lenin that he would have to move back a step. 'What it comes to,' he confessed, 'is this: the big cities and industrial centres were never in such a terrible situation as they are now, under this proletariat dictatorship.'

The party, after the defeat of the German Spartacists and the Jew-Communists of Buda-Pesth, began to realize that world-revolution was not one of to-morrow's fixtures. Lenin who exhibited a strange combination of the fierce, uncompromising prophet dreaming on things to come, with the practical, common-sense realist who took in all the needs of the moment, succeeded, in the teeth of strenuous opposition on Trotsky's part, in securing the adoption by the tenth party congress of a new economic policy, which, after its own initials, came to be known as the 'N.E.P.'

The *Nep*, which took many of the stricter Bolsheviks by surprise, harked back to a limited and controlled sort of capitalism. There was to be an end of rationing, and to confiscation, markets were to be re-opened, small producers were to be free to sell their goods.

This was to go retrograde with a vengeance, a very palpable rebuff! But Lenin understood that, if these concessions had not been granted, the Bolsheviks would never have remained in power, and he sacrificed strict economic orthodoxy in order to maintain the political supremacy of the party.

The establishment of the *Nep*, which meant the complete stultification of Lenin *qua* theorist, was, as it turned out, his last important decision. Some-time before, at a workers' social gathering, a young Jewish woman-student named Dora Kaplan had fired a revolver at him and inflicted a wound from which he had never properly recovered. At present his health, already impaired by this attempt, was becoming progressively worse. In May, 1922, he was attacked by some serious arterial trouble which left him partially paralysed, with no hope of recovery. He had only twelve more months to live.

This last year of his life was wholly occupied with his struggle against his coming successor. Stalin was a Georgian ex-terrorist, who, up till then, had only fulfilled roles of secondary importance. But having succeeded in getting himself appointed Secretary-General of the Party, he amplified his office with the most varied prerogatives. Seeing a vacancy approaching, Stalin began quietly and secretly to select the men of whom, when the day came, he would be able to make reliable tools. All the doubtful ones he sent into exile. From the others he exacted a promise of unconditional obedience.

A serious dispute broke out between Lenin and Stalin on the question of Georgia which, anxious to assume a menshevik autonomy, had put the Bolsheviks in a minority. At Stalin's instigation, the *Politbureau* censored one of Lenin's articles. The last letter which the sick man ever wrote was one breaking off all relations with Stalin. It was to be a fight to a finish — and a quick

finish at that. What would have come of it, if the quarrel
had gone on? What appalling scenes of bloodshed, what
fratricidal strife would have been added to the dreadful
toll of Russia's calamities? Anything might have happened. But Lenin succumbed to a fresh attack on the
21st January, 1924. His remains were embalmed and
at once became the object of official veneration, which
was useful, as it served the purpose of disguising the
repudiation in practice of all that he had maintained
in theory, a repudiation to which stern reality, mightier
even than his fanatic will, slowly but ineluctably compelled him.

STALIN

THE Leader dead, the struggle for power, all the more violent because it had to be secret, began among those of his disciples who, undaunted by ever growing difficulties, deemed themselves qualified to succeed him.

And it is true that if, on Lenin's death, the *Nep* did save Russia from an economic crisis of a magnitude never before known in Europe, (the famine of 1921 carried off nearly thirty millions), the situation of the country was still sufficiently deplorable. One half of the land which had been under cultivation in 1913 was now lying fallow. The value of the corn harvest was less than half of its pre-war figure. The price of manufactured articles was prohibitive, while wages were scarcely a third of what they were in 1914. The minor retail trade was in the hands of pedlars and hucksters. Millions of peasants, being unable to work for the big landowners, were deprived of all means of subsistence.

The bureaucracy had its four hundred thousand communist employees well paid and well housed, while in Moscow the overcrowding was so terrible that sometimes as many as ten people had to herd together in a single cellar. Such a contrast only made their misery the more intolerable.

Wages being several months in arrear, the workers had not the wherewithal to provide themselves with the barest necessities. Strikes broke out and Trotsky laid the blame on Stalin who had filled the government offices with his creatures, heedless of whether they were fit for the work or not, his sole demand being that they should serve his own personal ambitions. Such was the opening episode of a struggle that was destined to continue for six years. The Triumvirate (the Russians call it the Troika) of the *Politbureau*, viz. Stalin, Zinoviev and Kamenev, made up their mind that Trotsky must be shelved. If it took some time to accomplish that result, it was because Stalin realized that the hero of the 17th October was not the sort of man he could send packing like a head clerk.

After the congress of 1924 (the 13th!) which aimed at the unification of the Bolshevik party, Stalin's favourite purging activities were resumed with renewed vigour. All those 'comrades' who were disinclined to yield him servile obedience were excluded from the party, and went to swell the ranks of the twenty million unemployed.

There were risings, but they were quenched in a sea of blood. Police repression grew more and more severe throughout the country.

The quarrel between Trotsky and Stalin went on, watched with curious interest by the men in power. Trotsky was no match for his adversary in skill and cunning. His 'permanent revolution' dogma seemed particularly dangerous to Bolsheviks who had handsomely feathered their nests. He was merely looked on as an agitator of the Extreme Left in a country where opportunism pure and simple was regarded as the only acceptable policy. From 1926 onwards, the dubious people with whom he was allied, the disreputable

character of the men who formed his set, undermined his
prestige. Stalin, by cooking some of the documents,
contrived to minimize the role he had played in the
coup d'état and the civil war, awarding all the glory to
himself. Trotsky attempted to bring off a *coup de main*
in November, 1927, the tenth anniversary of the revolution, and failed. In 1928, he was exiled, and the
following year he withdrew to Turkey.

To reinforce his prestige, Stalin conceived the idea of
kindling the fires of revolt in China. But the *coups d'état*
carried out by the military in Shanghai, Pekin, Canton
and Nankin were a rude shock to his policy. All he had
done was to send some hundreds of Chinese workers to
their death. Any other European political leader would
have reeled under such a blow. Not so, Stalin. He could
count on the blind obedience of the Cheka to see to it
that he should be the one and only source of information.
Come what might, his shrewdness would be held up to
admiration.

His Jewish acolytes, Zinoviev and Kamanev, of whom
he now wanted to be rid and against whom he thought
of working up an anti-Semite agitation, saved their heads
by redoubling their obsequiousness and protestations of
allegiance. They capitulated all along the line. But
henceforth the posts assigned to them were of second-rate
importance. Stalin, on the other hand, got the Fourteenth Congress to appoint him life secretary of the party.
Feeling his position at last secure, he now thought himself able to put his economic theories into practice.

In 1928 he launched the Five Years' Plan.

The practical results of this plan, which was advertised

with unexampled prodigality, have failed to come up to expectations. What it has achieved is the fortuitous production of a few gigantic industrial concerns, which have afforded excellent propaganda material but have as yet served no useful purpose, because they have no connexion with the real needs of the Russian people.

One hundred and eighteen milliards of roubles have been swallowed up in producing results which, as the official statistics themselves bear witness, have only with the most painful effort achieved the half of what was expected of them in 1928. Almost everywhere the output of energy has been barren of result. The Turksib railway, which, be it observed, was begun under the old régime, is a case in point. Very few trains run at all, and those few are very slow. The Dnieprostzoï dam, the work of an American engineer, will go on turning its machinery *in vacuo* for many a year to come for lack of transformers and cables to transmit the current. At Nijni-Novgorod seventy-five per cent of the motor cars which the Ford factories are so busily turning out will be unusable in a country destitute of metalled roads. The delicate American machine-tools were soon put out of order in the factories and on farms, where the workers had not been trained in their use. An important undertaking consisting of iron foundries and blast furnaces called the Magnitorsk was established, but it was two thousand kilometres away from the coal mines. Hence the exorbitant price of the insignificant quantity of steel produced. The rest is all of a piece.

A tacit recognition of failure was implied in the spate of 'plans' which began to follow one after another without intermission. Since 1933 we have heard no more of them.

Officially, there is no unemployment. Fluctuations in the supply of labour, however, are admitted. They correspond with the wandering from place to place of millions of workers. These migrations of the proletariat are one of the glaring defects of the régime. Every possible means of coercion have been brought into play to prevent them. Workmen were given identity books like those given to soldiers. Residence in a given area was made compulsory. The passport system was introduced, but nothing availed to keep the working population in one place, and they continued to wander from town to town in search of conditions of life a little less pitiable, of a 'boss' a little less cruel. The unity of command which had been in force in the factories since 1929, had destroyed what few remaining shreds of liberty remained to the men. Henceforth they lived like convicts.

The schools programme had likewise proved a failure, notwithstanding all the fine hopes it had engendered. So far from diminishing, the number of illiterates became greater than ever.

Finally, all those who wielded the pen, journalists, novelists, historians, poets, were enjoined to praise the government without stint. If they did not, they were deported.

And that is where things are now. Stalin is a cunning politician but a man of limited vision, and no intellectual culture. In the realm of economics he has never brought any but elementary schoolboy ideas to the solution of the problems confronting him, solution that outrage the essential conditions of human existence for the sake of some impossible chimera.

Under his dictatorship, the Russian people are much worse off than they were before the war. They are obsessed by fears of food shortage, by the extreme difficulty of procuring for themselves the irreducible minimum requisite for bare subsistence. The beauty of Soviet rule may be gauged by the fact that it takes several days to obtain a railway ticket, and a whole afternoon to purchase a little sugar, that is, when there's any to purchase.

Universal collectivism has killed all individual initiative. The enthusiasm of a few cohorts of picked men specially trained and fed who are produced in order to impress distinguished visitors and the gentlemen of the foreign press, is not enough to make up for the apathy of an entire people plodding away without cessation and without hope at their allotted piece of prison-work.

It is calculated that in eleven years Stalin has driven five million peasants from their homes and sent as exiles to the islands of the White Sea, the Arctic Ocean, or the depths of Siberia between eight and ten millions of men of every class of society, soldiers, working men, civil servants, business men and intellectuals.

Having united in his own hands the various departments of state, exercising without control the power of life and death over the whole of Russia, Stalin comes before us like an Oriental despot, combined, as one of his adversaries has put it, with all the absurdities of Bouvard and Pecuchet.

But in his dictatorship, as in Lenin's, it is a long time

since the Russian Revolution has been anything more than a memory. Both of them started from the same old principle, that force is the midwife of social systems. The forceps, indeed, are particularly necessary when a monstrosity is to be delivered.

M. ATTATURK

FORMERLY MUSTAPHA KEMAL

AFTER the war, the victorious Allies were for setting up again the former 'Capitulations', whereby Europeans in the Ottoman Empire were released from the jurisdiction of the Turkish courts of Law. Thereupon, a Turkish delegate inquired, with a smile, 'Why do you want to treat us like savages? Here in this delegation, we are all doctors of law of the University of Paris.'

That sally throws a light on the extraordinary transformation wrought in a few years, in a country deemed unchangeable, by a leader of indomitable will who had imbued himself with the ideas of the intellectual *élite*. This is how it comes about, that among all the dictators of our time, the most curious and most original figure is perhaps that of Mustapha Kemal.

He has not Hitler's vogue, or Mussolini's, or even Stalin's. That is because our relations with Turkey, important as they have been down the ages, important as they still are, have not the urgency of our relations with Germany, Italy and Russia. It must, however, be admitted that, if a dictatorship is to be judged by the magnitude of the changes it has wrought in a country, there is not one among the newer governments which has been responsible for such a radical transformation as the government of Mustapha Kemal. From such a standpoint, this modern dictator, who aims at making his

country a European country, who invokes the example
of the French Revolution, who admires America and
aims at being in the forefront of his times, reminds us
very strongly of certain Eastern despots. There is
something equally reminiscent about him of Washington
and Gengis Khan. But clearly the man he most closely
resembles is Peter the Great, the Tzar who determined
to Europeanize Russia within a few years and compelled
the *boyards* to sacrifice their beards on pain of death.
Mustapha Kemal (Kemal signifies 'the Perfect One')
was born at Salonica in 1880. His origin is somewhat
obscure. Some say he is a pure-bred Anatolian, others
that he is a Macedonian, that is to say a cross between
a Slav and a Bulgarian, from a country containing a
greater mixture of races than any other in Europe.
Others, again, assert that he is an Albanian. Be that
as it may, he certainly comes of peasant stock. His father
was a customs agent and, later on, a dealer in timber.
He gave his son a fairly up-to-date education. After his
father's death, and in spite of his mother's opposition,
Mustapha entered the Military College. By 1904, he
was a staff-captain.

He was by this time greatly taken up with politics.
He dreamed high dreams as he thought sadly on his
country and the corruption and oppression under which
it laboured, and he began to conspire against the Sultan
Abdul-Hamed. He was sent off in disgrace to Damascus
and Salonica, and there he started some secret societies.
He was a Young Turk of the second generation, the
generation which deemed that the Salonica Revolution
had been abandoned too soon.

In 1914, he opposed Turkey's entry into the war on the side of Germany. However, he did his duty, held a command in the Caucasus and, (this time as General) in Mesopotamia. As to the German General Falkenhayn, who tried to corrupt him with money, he was not afraid to express to him his contempt for such tactics. Shelved for a time, he was at length given command of a group of armies at the very time when Turkey was clamouring for an armistice and when the Grand Vizier was beginning to sell his country to Great Britain. At this time, Mustapha was in Anatolia. He received orders to disband his troops. He refused, and set up in opposition to the Government at Constantinople, a government of his own at Angora, an uncomfortable but impregnable stronghold. He became the soul of the national resistance movement and General Gouraud, who had praised him highly, was not mistaken in his opinion.

All this happened just when Venizelos's Greeks, supported by Great Britain, were landing in Smyrna. Mustapha organized the defence, refused to obey Constantinople and, on the 21st January, 1921, declared that the sovereignty belonged to the nation and that the governing power was vested in the 'Great National Assembly'. At the same time he entered into an alliance with Moscow (while energetically putting down all Communist propaganda) and, in September, inflicted a defeat on the Greek army. In 1922 a new armistice was signed, and Mustapha received the name of El Ghazi, which signified 'The Victorious One'. On the 1st November, the Assembly, in session at Angora, deposed the Sultan and declared that the Khalifat should con-

tinue to be carried on by the Osman family, on condition
that the Assembly should have power to choose from
among its members the prince deemed worthy of that
honour. In 1923, Mustapha Kemal was elected 'President
of the Republic'.

Soon, however, he found it necessary to abolish the
Khalifat out of hand, proclaiming that religion was a
matter for the individual conscience. The world was
aghast. It was feared that the whole of Islam would cry
out against it. In the event, only a few Indian Moslem
communities made any protest. The remainder, who
from time immemorial had been divided by their
various heresies, were not excessively moved at seeing the
fictitious authority of the Commander of the Believers
brought to an end. Thus the separation of Church and
State was accomplished. It is somewhat curious to
observe that, in all countries and in all times, it is with
religion that dictators first concern themselves.

Mustapha's avowed ambition, after his victories, after
repressing the Kurdish insurrection and saying good-bye
to England, who had become too interfering by half, was
to convert Turkey, a large part of whose European
territories he had succeeded, by the Treaty of Lausanne,
in preserving, into a country on the same footing as the
other Western powers. And what is the first step towards
such equality? Why, to present the same outward appearance; not to exhibit any differences in the way of
dress. The world arrives at equality by way of uniformity.
And so, like all other Orientals, he deemed that the first
battle to fight was the battle of the tailors and hatters.
All young Chinamen pride themselves on having put off

their pig-tails and on wearing cloth caps or trilbys. Mustapha the Victorious decided to abolish the fez, he also had to 'abolish' the heads of some score or so of obstinate die-hards.

The battle of the hats was perhaps the hardest he had ever had to fight. Moslems do not uncover the head in their mosques. The fez having no brim, is convenient, inasmuch as it allows the wearer to touch the ground with his forehead, and it is never in the way. Mustapha made a large number of speeches in his campaign advocating an international mode of dress for all civilized nations. The town of Brusa in an outburst of enthusiasm, abjured the fez, but having no stock of hats to draw on, decided to go bare-headed pending the arrival of supplies. At Erzeroum on the other hand the inhabitants revolted. However, little by little things calmed down. The Turks consented to live bare-headed before God and their betters, and to wear hats in the street.

At the same time Mustapha did away with the *petche* and the *tchartchaff*, that is to say with the Turkish robe and the veil with which the women hid their faces. For some considerable time the fight for the emancipation of women had been going on. The example had been set by the Soviet Republics in the Caucasus with their Moslem population, and in particular by the Republic of Azerbeidjan which had been independent for two years, and which claimed the glorious distinction of being the first Islamic Republic. It had given its women the vote. Mustapha did not go to that length, but he did away with the segregation of the sexes at public entertainments and in railway trains. He authorized

and encouraged Turkish women to go on the stage; he
permitted them to dance in public with strangers.
If political emancipation was still to come, social
emancipation was already an accomplished fact.

Of that there is one outstanding proof, the abolition of
polygamy. Mustapha spoke of the famous book of Islam
with derision. He tossed it on to the scrap heap. The
Turkish Civil Code was based on the Koran. Mustapha,
having separated the temporal power from the spiritual,
looked about for a Code sufficiently up-to-date to be
applied to Turkey. In 1926, without a debate, and by
an enactment consisting of a single clause, the Swiss
Code (which dates from 1912) was unanimously adopted
by the National Assembly. In order to avoid endless
discussions, it was agreed to as it stood. He also introduced divorce and civil marriage.

Furthermore, the Ghazi proceeded to set on foot a
number of social reforms: a code regulating the hours
and conditions of labour, a weekly rest day, Sunday
being fixed upon instead of Friday, which was the day
sanctified by the Koran, the abolition of the dime.
As we are aware he has recently made the adoption of
the Latin alphabet and the Gregorian calendar compulsory in Turkey. It will be seen that one could
hardly break more completely with the past. In his
anxiety to imitate, and indeed to outdo, the Western
nations, Mustapha Kemal has just issued a decree for
the introduction of wireless into the most out-of-the-way
villages. Nothing he could think of for putting old
Turkey out of existence, has he left undone. A country
which had the reputation of being immovable he has

endowed with the rapidity of the cinema. He turns out reforms as if they were being reeled off a film.

However, strong nations have a habit of clinging to their past. And here it is that Mustapha's attitude is the most remarkable. At the time of the struggle with the Greeks, the Turks had made an oath, before the mosque of Ahmed, to fight to the death. They had invoked the glories of ancient Islam. After the break with the Khalifat and Koranic customs had become final, Mustapha Kemal tried to sever every remaining link with the Osman princes. Whereas for a European the past history of Turkey is one with the past history of the Sultans, Mustapha Kemal had new history books compiled in which the story of centuries is compressed into twenty pages.

However, as it would be foolish to date the genesis of this great nation from the war of 1914, our modern dictator has set about providing it with a more illustrious ancestry than the wandering tribes of Turkestan from which it is descended. It happened at the moment that several archaeological bodies had unearthed important remains of the Hittite civilization. The Hittites were not unknown. There was no doubt that they had invaded Egypt, and that the daughters of the Pharoahs had sometimes united themselves in wedlock with the princes of that race. The Bible contains allusions to their Empire. The ruins discovered in Anatolia, the gigantic statues which recall the art of Crete or Mexico, seem to suggest the existence of a mighty kingdom. Mustapha Kemal annexed the Hittites and caused their history to be disseminated, though it must be admitted that it raises more problems than it solves. A little later, an era yet more remote was explored and the Sumerians were brought to light. After this, Sumerians became the fashion, the great Turkish Bank called itself the 'Sumerian Bank', and several important personages, when invited to choose an hereditary appellation (another leaf out of the European book) adopted that of Sumer. As regards himself, Mustapha Kemal is henceforth to be known as Monsieur Attaturk.

But the most extraordinary reform to which this amazing dictator has addressed himself is the linguistic one. Turkish is not a pure language and Arabic and Persian words are frequently met with in it. To start with, the use of this language was made compulsory, even in the sphere of religion. The Arabic Koran was translated into Turkish; so were the liturgical books. The next step was to purify it.

The introduction of the Roman alphabet had already made a number of words unusable. To replace them a Commission, presided over by Mustapha Kemal, proceeded to carry out researches among the local dialects, in ancient texts and even in the *patois* of Turkestan. Gradually everything of Arabian or Persian origin was banished from the Turkish language. What is so remarkable about all this is that the entire nation entered with zest into labours without precedent in history. People cudgelled their brains to discover new words, or to revive old forms of expression. Thus, slowly and surely, a new language is being evolved.

Of course it has its drawbacks. Two years ago, the death occurred of a great poet who, such is the respect paid by the government and the people to their national idols, was accorded a magnificent funeral. But it was confessed that the younger folk could not make much out of his verses, which were written in 'pre-war Turkish' and which, ten years hence, will probably have to be translated.

On the other hand, just two months ago the official dictionary of the new language was given to the world. Within a few days the early editions were sold out and some mischievous wags said the reason was obvious; nobody knows anything about New Turkish, a purely artificial creation, that has to be learnt as one would learn Esperanto.

At any rate this strange and rather terrifying experiment is certainly the most original of all Mustapha Kemal's reforms. It shows us how constructive, how creative is the dictator's mind, even when he has all the ingrained habits and customs of national life arrayed against him.

However, it is abundantly clear that the Turk, despite the 'modern' aspect of these reforms, puts up with them with exactly the same passivity with which he would put up with any extravagant ordinance that an Asiatic autocrat might impose upon him. This mixture of Oriental despotism and Western imitativeness it is that makes this Ghazi a figure so unique.

There is nothing he cannot permit himself, and the gaze of all the East is upon him, notwithstanding his defiance of the Koran. There is an aureole of legend about him. It is given out that he lives in a continuous whirl of gaiety, that he spends his nights dancing and making merry, going straight from the tavern to regulate the finances of the country or to busy himself with some up-to-date scheme of town-planning. Who knows but that, when twenty more years have elapsed, he may be looked on as the last of the Sultans ?

At any rate he makes it clear that a powerful dictator can make a nation do almost anything he wishes, and, whether they like it or not, change their habits and their mode of life at a day's notice.

I do not think this mode of introducing reforms would be popular among the French. The leaders of the revolution tried to change the names of the months, but, musical as the new names were, the experiment proved a failure.

MUSSOLINI AND FASCISM

OF all the nations of the world, the Italians yield to none in the readiness with which they grasp the salient necessities of a political situation. A deep historic sense, a recollection of great deeds of the past, provide them with an unfailing source of motives for present action. This evocation of the past has never ceased to fire the Italian imagination. It is still enough of a living force for the Italians of to-day to draw inspiration from the examples set them by their forefathers in times long past.

The politicians of the old school, whose perceptions had been laid asleep throughout the long years during which, in Italy as elsewhere, the parliamentary system held the field, failed to notice the re-emergence of this deep-rooted national sentiment. Their failure so to do sealed the doom of their régime and prepared the way for the wave of popular revolution which was to bear them irresistibly from the scene.

It is impossible to understand the genesis of Fascism unless one bears in mind that, in 1915, Italy came into the war after a fierce conflict between 'neutralists' and 'interventionists'. The 'interventionists' had carried the day. D'Annunzio, the poet, had triumphed over the crafty Giolitti.

After the final victory, the neutralists, who had remained in office, thought that things would continue in the old rut. But they were destitute now alike of credit and authority. They could no longer command respect, or exact obedience. They were indeed allied with all the forces of disorder. No government can succeed in its task if it allies itself with the baser against the higher elements of the nation. Anarchy increased. The State, 'democratico-liberal' as it was ticketed, was falling to pieces. Italy was ripe for a despotism, whether Bolshevist or Nationalist. All that remained was to find out who was to give the 'knock-out blow to the paralytic', that is, to the existing régime.

From that instinct of self-preservation which is common to all men, whether as individuals or as members of a nation, was born Fascism, a weapon of resistance against the forces of death by which Italy was menaced.

This reaction, which had failed to assert itself in the Russia of 1916, sprang, in Italy, from historic sentiment, from memories of ancient Rome and of those dictatorships set up in hours of peril which have always been looked upon as distinctly Roman. But, as a matter of fact, Fascism was not a thing called into being on the spur of the moment. At the time of the March on Rome, it was exactly eight years since Mussolini had begun preparing to take the government into his own hands.

Benito Mussolini was the son of a village blacksmith who was also a militant socialist. Benito had always wanted to be a teacher, and at sixteen behold him a schoolmaster! As he seasoned his lessons with not a little revolutionary propaganda, it was not long before he found himself out of work, a circumstance which did not increase his love of the bourgeoisie.

In order to earn his daily bread he emigrated to Switzerland, where, among other callings, he practised that of mason, still retaining his interest in politics. So little concerned was he to conceal his subversive opinions that the Federal authorities forbade him residence in certain cantons. As the hint only served to stimulate his activities, he was at last compelled to quit the country.

His experiences as a militant socialist had already enabled him to recognize the existence of two sorts of revolutionaries: those who work for the revolution, and those who use it as a means to secure their own advancement and personal gain. Being passionately devoted to ideas, he felt the most unmitigated disgust for those latter, whom he calls 'the parasites' of the social struggle. His aversion to politicians dates from this point.

A son of the people, one who had drunk deep of the cup of Marxian doctrines, his dream was to redeem the proletariat from bourgeois domination and to win for them a higher standard of living. After completing his Army service with the *bersaglieri* of Verona, where he came more than once under the rigours of military discipline, a sort of intellectual expansion compelled him again to quit his native land. His instinct led him to the Irridento, to Opaglia in the Trentino which at that time was still in the possession of Austria. It was there that he fell in with the man who was to change the whole course of his destiny. His name was Cesare Battisti.

A socialist like Mussolini, Battisti was consumed with patriotic fervour.

The Austrians, when they hanged him, probably fulfilled his dearest wishes; he would have glimpsed a promise of victory in the aureole of martyrdom. Born at Trent, he had spent all his student days in Florence. When thereafter he returned to his native soil, his dwelling became a centre of fervent nationalism. Possessed of knowledge at once infinitely deeper and more extensive than his new companion could boast of, he put the finishing touches on Mussolini's intellectual development and persuaded him that his social ideas were perfectly compatible with his longing for a greater Italy, if indeed they were not the very means to obtain it.

This blend of nationalism and socialism is Mussolini's distinctive characteristic. It affords the key to all his actions.

Battisti gave his disciple the hospitality of a Trent newspaper, the *Popolo*, of which he was editor. Mussolini gave vent to opinions of such violence that he was soon expelled by the police. But his homecoming from Austria was very different from his homecoming from Switzerland. Mussolini was warmly welcomed by the socialists of Milan, who entrusted him with the editorship of their paper, *Avanti*. On Battisti's advice, Mussolini started a campaign urging the Socialist party to take over the Government, for he believed he saw in Socialism an instrument of national recovery. From 1912 to 1914, he worked hard at organizing the working classes and urged them to attack the bourgeoisie with all the energy at their command. He was an agitator of the Karl Marx school, but he was also a patriot, and he refused to be at the beck and call of an International.

In June, 1914, he thought he saw his chance. During a riot which broke out at Ancona, three working men were killed by the police. In a few days the whole of the working-class population of Italy was up in arms. Nearly everywhere a general strike was proclaimed and there were some serious disorders. It only needed a call to fight the good fight and the forces of revolution would be masters of the land. Mussolini, feeling confident of victory, insisted that the movement should be followed up. But to his stupefaction the party leaders refused to support him. They drew the line at an appeal to violence. And more than that, the labour organizations, who had been skilfully got at by the 'parasites', decided on a resumption of work. The old bourgeoisie and their government had won the day.

Hardly had Mussolini had time to give vent to his indignation at the socialist leaders' treachery than the Great War broke out. Not only did the patriot feel a thrill, but the socialist as well. War alone could deliver from bondage the lands that had been sundered from the fatherland. Social emancipation also it would bring perforce, for a breath from the spirit of revolution has life in it, whereas books only breathe the odour of death.

From the very beginning the editor of *Avanti* was for intervention. He was urged along that path by Battisti. Battisti, too, had grasped the significance of the conjuncture, and as an irredentist his patriot blood was set on fire. From within the ranks of the socialist party they entered on a fierce campaign for the abandonment of neutrality.

Again, as in June, Mussolini's activities were held up by the theorists and politicians of his party, who had remained faithful to German social-democracy. Then his anger broke forth. He raged furiously against the emasculated 'idea-mongers' who were capable of sacrificing this unique chance of realizing Italian nationalist ideals, for the sake of their dogmas.

In October, at the socialist congress at Bologna, he delivered a violent speech, calling for intervention. In order to shut his mouth, the socialist pontiffs deprived him of the editorship of the newspaper *Avanti*. In this way, they thought that, being robbed of his platform, he would be less dangerous. To this move, Mussolini replied by founding a new paper entitled symbolically the *Popolo d'Italia* with the sub-title, 'Socialist Daily'.

This act of open rebellion entailed his definite removal from the party. On the previous occasion, he had presented his defence before a tumultuously enthusiastic assembly. Now, when he appeared in the tribune, he was greeted with shouts of 'Down with Mussolini!' He retained his calm and, having explained his reasons and his hopes, he concluded pathetically 'I declare to you that, from this time forth, to all hypocrites and all cowards, I shall show no quarter, no pity. If you think you are going to exclude me from public life, you are mistaken. You will find me confronting you, a living and implacable antagonist.'

That same night, he wrote in his diary '*The Mussolini case is not finished. It has just begun*'.

On his banishment from the party, that is to say during the final weeks of 1914, Mussolini founded the organization of Fascists. By January, 1915, he had gathered round him five thousand adherents. The programme of the Fascists was simple. It was by all possible means to bring Italy into the war against the Central Empires. Side by side with the nationalist D'Annunzio, and the syndicalist Corradoni, Mussolini the socialist carried on the fiery campaign which culminated in a declaration of war on Austria.

The leader of the Fascists hailed it as a deliverance. In him, though he had not taken note of it, the nationalist strain had assumed the mastery over the socialist. On the 22nd May, 1915, the day of the Italian mobilization, he wrote as follows: 'We have lived through these latter years in an atmosphere of general contempt and commiseration. Now the hour to make good all our claims has sounded, the hour which will mark the beginning of a new era for our country, a mighty testing time after which, once we have recovered confidence in ourselves, we shall become the equals of the other nations engaged in the battle of the future and the competition for work.' Next day, the day war was declared, he uttered this cry of pure and passionate affection for his country. 'For thy sake, O Italy, our mother, without fear and without regret, we are ready to live and die.'

Destiny came within a hair's breadth of taking him at his word. When serving as a corporal in a regiment of *bersaglieri*, Mussolini, in February, 1917, was wounded in twenty-four places by the explosion of a hand-grenade.

Being now unfit for service at the front, he resumed the editorship of his *Popolo d'Italia*, and continued the struggle against the defeatists of every kind who wanted

Italy to sign a shameful peace. He also had it in mind to regroup the Fascists who had been dispersed by the mobilization.

The events of October, 1917, the Caporetto disaster, went like iron into his soul, but he was one of those who refused to despair. 'We mean to win, we must win and we shall win', he wrote on the 2nd November. And, day in day out, until the armistice of Vittorio Veneto, he encouraged the faint-hearted and rallied the waverers.

Nowhere was Italy's dissatisfaction with the terms of peace so keenly felt as in the little group of friends that surrounded Mussolini. In 1919, the economic situation was deplorable. The socialist organizations, anxious to make capital out of the prevailing misery and discontent, profoundly impressed by the Russian experiment in revolution and encouraged by the pusillanimity of the Orlando government, incited the populace to strike, to riot and destroy.

The men who had been through the war were demobilized without any flourish of trumpets. Many of the home-comers found it the most difficult matter in the world to get work. The peasants had been promised that plots of land should be theirs, but all they saw for their pains was an unproductive market for their goods and a situation worse than before the war.

No sooner was he back again in the bosom of his family, than it began to dawn on him that the men who had fought in the war were the victims of a colossal swindle. Ex-service men were filled with a silent but stubborn hatred of the ruling class and of the politicians, who fell back again into the old rut and displayed a lamentable incapacity to reap any benefit from the victory won. The contrast between a soldier's life, between the daily sacrifice of field and firing-line and the moral suffocation which the events of 1919 inflicted on young Italy, was too great not to provoke one of those violent dislocations which are so fruitful a source of revolution.

Mussolini felt all this, as he felt how Labour, more and more worked up by Moscow propaganda, was seething with discontent. But be it as revolutionary as it might, that sort of revolution, the communist sort, was not what he wanted at all. He knew what would be the outcome of that — Italy would sink, never to rise again. What had to be done was to get the two revolutionary currents to flow in one and the same direction, the 'ex-service man' current and the 'popular current', to take the lead of both and then to merge them in one and the same movement. As early as the Spring of 1919 the *Popolo d'Italia* set to work to bring about getting them together. At the very outset, Mussolini stated the problem clearly and sharply. 'We have', he said, 'no need to await the revolution, like the herd of party ticket-holders. Nor are we afraid of the word, like the poor timid creatures whose ideas are just where they were in 1914. Why, we've been through our revolution already, we went through it in 1915.'

By thus reminding them of the interventionist campaign, he compelled the attention of the ex-soldiers, and by speaking of revolution as a thing to be desired, he also won a hearing from the malcontents, who insisted that it was time things changed.

In order to make his object clearer still, the sub-title

of *il Popolo* was changed. The 'Socialist Daily' became 'The Workers' and Ex-service Men's Journal'. On the 6th March, 1919, Mussolini announced that he was about to form a new political association which would afford a common rallying ground for all who laboured under a grievance.

'On the 23rd March,' he wrote, 'there will come into being the opposition, the militant Fascists (the word *revolutionary* had disappeared) who will set themselves to cope with two dangers: one, which arises from the fear of change, that is the Right. The other, whose aim is destruction, that is the Left.'

He obtained five hundred supporters. At the first meeting of the Fascists, less than a hundred and fifty people were present: officers, writers, students, peasants with opinions varying from fierce nationalism to fervent trades unionism. It was a perfect microcosm of what the Fascist troops were afterwards to become.

The entire press, with the exception of one solitary newspaper, boycotted the meeting. The congressmen, returning to their homes, set to work in earnest. Each of them gathered in one or two or three friends or fellow workmen, and this formed the embryo of the movement. A campaign of intensive propaganda was developed and had a magnificent send off in the occupation of Fiume by d'Annunzio. While the press as a whole were sitting on the fence, *il Popolo* definitely approved the occupation of the town. The effect was immediate. The young nationalist opposition at once rallied to the Fascists. By October the first Fascist congress announced that one hundred and thirty seven branches had been formed with a total

215

membership of 20,395. This had been brought about in six months. The political disintegration of Italy was destined enormously to increase these figures.

As a result of the elections held on the 16th November, 1919, there were returned 156 socialists, 100 *popolari* or Christian democrats, 30 radicals, 8 republicans and 220 liberals. Mussolini, who stood for Milan, did not get in. The 'Reds' made sure they would soon be in power.

On the 3rd December a general strike was again declared. People were killed in the streets of all the big towns. Anarchy was at its height, the army was attacked in its barracks, officers were assaulted in broad daylight. Government after government resigned, after vainly endeavouring to cope with disturbances that grew graver every moment, fanned and fomented as they were with funds from Moscow. From July till half-way through September, Ancona, Leghorn, Milan and Bologna were the scenes of bloody riots in which scores of people were killed and hundreds wounded. In the country districts, the ringleaders of the revolution went about commandeering money and victuals from peasants and landlords, massacring and maltreating all who refused to hand over their savings and their stock.

It was in vain that appeals were made to Rome. The ministers refused to interfere. In Parliament they lay low, and — talked. The *lira* kept falling, the cost of living went up. Everyone wondered what would be the end of it.

On the 29th August, 1920, the Italian Metallurgical Federation gave orders to its members to occupy the works; the first step towards the great night. On the morning of the 30th the occupation began and the red flag was hoisted on the top of the lightning conductors. The managers and engineers, together with their families, were placed under guard, to serve as hostages. The strikers then proceeded to organize defences. A network of barbed wire was put up, trenches were dug from which the royal troops could be fired on. Every industry had its soviet, small-arms shops were looted, and stocks of rifles and ammunition collected. It was a fight to a finish.

The government made no move, or, if it did, it was in the wrong direction, as at Genoa, for example, where the military, on being attacked, fired on the crowd and were punished for defending themselves.

The revolution triumphed, bringing in its train its customary toll of suffering and bloodshed. The only opposition it encountered was put up by the Fascists. Not numerous enough to engage in pitched battles, they had recourse to guerilla tactics, in the country districts first of all, where they helped the peasants to resist the exactions of the 'red tyrants', and then in the larger centres of population, where, with well-chosen propaganda, they spared no effort to stir up honest folk to action.

But propaganda was not their only weapon. Wherever they saw a chance, they would follow it up with a well-prepared and neatly planted blow. Their adversaries realized that they were the most dangerous of their foes, and it was against them that all their defensive measures were directed. There was a ruthless hunting of Blackshirts. From the end of 1920 onwards, not a week went by but there was a clash between Fascists and Revolutionaries, sometimes a mere skirmish, sometimes a battle-royal. The list of slaughtered Fascists grew longer, but every such victim brought to the cause for which he died an added strength, a brighter fame. The roll of the Fascists rapidly increased.

The Fascist movement made daily progress because it had at last come to be recognized that it alone could prevent the complete Bolshevization of Italy.

Mussolini and his earlier comrades must have put in some terrific work in organizing a movement which, from the beginning of 1921 onwards, assumed such astounding proportions. In the April of that year, the regional congress was held at Emilia and 20,000 Black-shirts marched past their leader, hailing him with cheers. At Ferrara, two days later, 50,000 Fascist peasants carried him in triumph shoulder high. Fascism which originated with a few, was now a people's movement.

All it needed was a vantage ground from which its teaching could be propounded, its appeals made audible, its programme made clear, without any possibility of its being made the victim of a conspiracy of silence. The Government, quite unwittingly, proffered it such a vantage-ground — Parliament!

The premier, Giolitti, having resolved on an appeal to the country, thirty-five Fascist deputies were returned. Mussolini, who was elected both at Milan and Bologna, led the little band.

He at once proved himself a skilful parliamentarian. Though his principles admitted no compromise, he was moderate in his expression of them, and, though he made no promises, he contrived to win the support of all

patriots, Catholics and unbelievers, royalists and republicans.

In the Chamber, as well as outside of it, 'the Country'
was the rallying cry. In face of the growing peril, each
and all sacrificed their interests to the welfare of Italy.

More important even than this, a whole group of the
socialist troops, discouraged by the attitude of those in
authority over them, began to call to mind how full of
energy that old comrade of theirs had been, the comrade
who had now become the leader of the Fascists. And
they began to ask themselves whether he was not the
man to bring about the emancipation of the proletariat.
Mussolini, who had been kept well informed of this trend
of feeling, saw how all-important it was. The Fascist
troops might see their numbers doubled at a stroke and
the Fascist influence become predominant in the State.
That being so, he did not hesitate. On the 3rd August,
he signed a sort of treaty of peace with the socialists and
the Italian Labour headquarters. A good many Fascists,
not realizing what was in their leader's mind, took umbrage at this move. But Mussolini stood his ground and
at last prevailed on them to ratify his decision, with the
result that the socialists came over in a body. The
Government looked on helplessly as this *imperium in
imperio* came into being.

In view of the amplitude of the movement, the somewhat rough and ready organization of the militant Fascists had to be put on a more formal basis, with a regular
hierarchy of ranks and grades. This was the object of
the congress which began at Rome in October. Even
at that date there was something of the dictator about

Mussolini as he stood there, the supreme head of 2,200 Fascist groups comprising a total of 310,000 registered members, the majority of them under thirty.

The programme of the party was distributed by the million. It may be summed up briefly as follows:

Reform of the State by decentralization. Restriction of Parliamentary terms of reference to problems concerning the individual as a citizen of the State, the State being the organ for the realization and protection of the supreme interests of the nation; the creation of a system of corporations; restoration of the interior prestige of the State; affirmation of Italy's rights to her complete historical and geographical unity, even where that unity was not yet fully attained; recognition of the rights of private property; social measures requisite to bring about the extinction of class warfare by the legal recognition of workers' and employers' unions with the responsibilities arising therefrom; measures of all kinds designed to insure to all those towards whom the State had contracted a liability, such as ex-service men, men permanently disabled, civil servants, the due fulfilment of its liability.

Thus, over against a central power which was becoming progressively demoralized, the National Fascist Party rose up with a programme of practical reforms calculated to satisfy every son of Italy who was not prepared to acquiesce in his country's downfall.

In this year of grace 1922, government after government collapsed like a house of cards. The King had all the difficulty in the world to find men who would undertake to form a Cabinet. The crisis which followed on after Bonomi's government, on the 2nd February, lasted three weeks and a day. Such a spectacle of impotence brought crowds of adherents to the Fascist party. Both the Right and the Left were now equally convinced that any attempt to solve the problem by constitutional means was doomed to failure.

Meanwhile, the Fascists were not going to content themselves with a mere *pro forma* opposition. Wherever they could, they took the place of the defaulting public authority, thus impressing themselves on the popular imagination and making good their influence over the masses. In point of fact they were already masters of the situation.

However, such troops as still remained loyal to the parties of the extreme left, were in no mood as yet to abandon the struggle. The truce between Mussolini and Turati was now to all intents and purposes a dead letter. Not a day went by without some fresh outrage being attempted. The Fascists replied with their famous punitive expeditions. Moreover, they did not hesitate to occupy whole towns with a view to protecting the inhabitants from the activities undertaken by the socialists who wanted to wipe out their previous defeats. The Facta Government, finding itself unequal to the task of forcibly preventing these large-scale gatherings, pretended to ignore them, secretly hoping that some lucky turn of events would rid them of these turbulent Facisti. The Facta cabinet fell on the 19th July. From then, until the 1st August, Italy was without a government.

The Socialists played their last card on the 31st July when, once again, they declared a general strike. Mussolini's reply came like a thunderbolt. He mobilized all his Fascists and issued the following ultimatum:

'We give the government forty-eight hours in which to make good its authority in the eyes of those who are dependent upon it and of those who would strike at the very existence of the nation; failing which the Fascists will assume full liberty of action and put themselves in the place of a government that has demonstrated its incapacity.

Fascists of all Italy, rally to our side!'

All over the country, the Fascists took the place of the strikers. Order reigned in the big towns, thanks to the vigilance of the Blackshirt patrols. Those who attempted any counter-demonstration were thrashed within an inch of their lives. Before the week was out the strike had been broken. Fascists had eliminated socialism's last forces from the struggle. The malcontents themselves had lost faith in their leaders and a number of them rallied to the Fascists, discovering many an old companion among their ranks.

From that day, parliamentary government was definitely discredited. Signor Facta vainly attempted to form a new cabinet. Mussolini spoke strongly and to the point. 'We are tired', said he, 'of seeing Italy governed by men who are for ever oscillating between negligence and cowardice.'

The Government's reply was to offer Mussolini a seat in the Cabinet. They were willing to give the Fascists a post or two without portfolio and a few under-secretaryships. Mussolini declined. He demanded the Foreign Office, the War Office, the Admiralty, Labour and Public Works. He added that he was strong enough to take them. And he was.

At Naples it is a veritable army that marches past beneath his eyes, an army wild with enthusiasm. 'To Rome!' 'To Rome!' shout the legions, pointing the way with clenched fists. The hour is striking; the hour which the Duce (the name his troops have given him) has been waiting for these twenty years. Back once more in Milan, he sends a message to Facta who is sinking ever deeper and deeper into the Parliamentary quagmire. It is an ultimatum and it gives him forty-eight hours to resign. Facta makes a feeble attempt at resistance. A few guns are placed on Monte Mario, and the bridges over the Tiber are barred with *chevaux de frise*. The King hurries back from San Rossoro. From every side the news comes pouring in that the Fascist columns are on the march to Rome. Facta implores the King to sign a decree proclaiming martial law. Victor Emmanuel will do no such thing. He knows what Fascism stands for. He knows that Italy's future lies there. Two days later, on the 29th October, 1922, Benito Mussolini is sent for to the Quirinal. Thither, from Milan, he hastens with all speed, and is requested by the King to form a government. Fascism is coming into its own.

Since then, the story of Mussolini's dictatorship is too well known to require anything more than a summary of the essential facts. A victorious encounter with the *popolari*; the 1924 elections, when the Fascists obtained five million votes against their opponents' two million; the Matteoti affair which gave a serious jolt to the new régime; the break with Parliament and the liberal ministry, which culminated in the famous circular of the 6th January, 1927, Mussolini's first appearance as an absolute dictator. With a stroke of the pen (well supported by bayonets) this circular swept all opposition from his path.

Wielding an authority comparable to that of the dictators of ancient Rome, the Duce devoted all his power to the regeneration of his country. In politics he is a realist, and, in his contact with realities, he has discarded whatever may have been too elaborately theoretical in his mental equipment. He has so modified his ideas as to make them square with the necessities of a living policy.

In thirteen years, Mussolini brought about a profound change in Italy, transforming her into the great power which even the most ambitious of her sons scarcely dared to imagine.

This process of restoration was applied in all the various departments of public life — political, economic, social, maritime, military. A whole nation was its artisan, for it could only have been accomplished by sacrifices on the part of all, freely conceded. As Mussolini himself wrote in 1932, 'Life, as Fascism understands it, must be earnest, austere, religious, and based on moral strength.' That force exists. No one can deny it. It has taken on an almost religious form, and that is not without its dangers.

The more one studies, with the attention and sympathy one owes to noble undertakings, the rise of the Italian Dictator, the more we must hope that this great wave of national enthusiasm will not blind him, in the end, to those perils to which a revolution is particularly exposed, and Fascism is, first and foremost, a revolution. Those who want France to follow suit, will do well to think twice about it. The 'Corporative Economy' devised by Mussolini would be regarded as monstrous by our middle class and our traders, big and small. Before we think about copying a thing, we ought to know exactly what it is we are going to copy. The Gallic cock is not designed by nature to suck the dugs of the Roman wolf.

PRIMO DE RIVERA

OR THE DICTATORSHIP THAT FAILED

THE fruitful policy of neutrality pursued by Spain in the European war, brought about a prosperity greater than she had known for several centuries. But making money is one thing. Keeping it another. That is a truth which the Spaniards, who committed the error of investing their profits in Germany, realized to their cost when, as a result of the catastrophic slump in German marks, they found themselves some four thousand million pesetas out of pocket.

Almost between sunset and sunrise, things in general had become much less easy, and the grievous disappointments of this grim period produced in their turn a moral and social cataclysm.

We beheld the efflorescence of a sort of 'gangsterism', particularly at Barcelona, in Catalonia, which, being a great industrial city, harbours a variety of elements which always take kindly to revolution, or, more properly, to anarchy.

About the year 1922, a government of politicians of the old school, Señores Santiago Alba, now President of the Cortes, and Garcia Prieto, had, owing to their easy-going liberalism and to their getting themselves involved in an entanglement with the Left, made it completely impossible for them to offer any resistance to the forces of disorder. The government's weakness left the country powerless to face up to the threats and premonitory symptoms of the revolution to come.

In the year 1923 alone, three hundred and twenty employers were assassinated in Catalonia. The Governor of Barcelona and the Archbishop of Saragossa shared the same fate.

These organized massacres called for punitive measures by the military which were carried out under the leadership of General Martinez Anido, an energetic man who unfortunately lacked the faculty of asserting his authority. He restricted himself to a few reprisals, and had not the nerve to put an end to a régime that was rotten from top to bottom. The cause of the trouble continued to exist.

Such was the position when, in September, 1923, General Primo di Rivera, Captain-General of Catalonia, in concurrence with other generals, Berenguer, Saro, Daban, the Duke of Tetuan, the Marquis Cavalcanti and the greater part of the army, decided to strike a sudden blow.

From 1920 to 1923 Primo de Rivera at Valencia and Barcelona had looked on at the progress of terrorism and the growing apathy of the government. The assassination of a non-commissioned officer by a young soldier under orders for Morocco, as a protest against the war in that country, had made it necessary to suspend the embarkation of the troops. This was the last straw. As a soldier he found it more than he could stand.

Primo issued a manifesto to all the Captains-General in the Peninsula, as well as an appeal to the nation. On the 14th September he left Barcelona and arrived at Madrid. The King, who went to the station to meet him, requested him to form a government.

As often happens, he found it easier to seize the position than to maintain it. He had successfully effected his surprise; now he was surprised in turn, for he felt from the very beginning that, if he was a staunch fighting man, he was a very indifferent administrator.

Primo de Rivera has been very aptly described as a mild dictator with a rough tongue. He was at once full of geniality and impatient of contradiction. He said himself that he was for a 'liberal dictatorship', as if the two words were not mutually exclusive.

The truth was, he had no ideas to go on, and no clear notion where he was making for, still less what he wanted to make for, and he had no confidence in himself. As a dictator he was altogether too gentlemanly, too refined.

It is reported that Mussolini, at the first interview he had with the General, told him it was a pity he had begun by saying his dictatorship was only temporary. He might also have blamed him still more, since it was perhaps his most grievous failing, for not having fired the national imagination, for having been too much of a materialist. The strong men of our day, the men that carry the country along with them, are nationalists. But nationalism, at all events at that juncture, was not Spain's strong point.

For the rest, Primo was an Andalusian, with all the qualities and all the defects of his race. Charm, intelligence, wit, address, these no one could deny him; but they were counter-balanced by a carelessness, a free and

easy scepticism, by no means suited to a statesman
called upon to guide the ship of State. He somewhat
resembled the *tcreros* of his native country. When the
bull-fight is over, all they think about is love-making.

A very fine *catallero*, in the Castilian sense of the word,
he was rather too *cavalier*, as the French understand it.
He could speak and he could write with equal facility,
and as he himself wrote newspaper articles, official
notices and government decrees, straight off, without
ever pausing to read them over, the facility was not
without its drawbacks.

He was a soldier, with a soldier's virtues and a soldier's
faults. Courage, honour, probity, rectitude — all the
qualities which go to the making of an exemplary soldier
we may freely grant him, for he gave himself to the service
of his king and country till he had no more to give.

But — it is useless to deny it — ideas were not his
strong point. His work always remained on the material
level; he never touched men's hearts and minds. He
never gained a hearing from the intellectuals of his
country and, despite his good intentions, never managed
to overcome the unpopularity with which the younger
University folk regarded his administration. Now, for
good or ill, that is where revolutions generally begin.
You don't conquer ideas by clapping them into irons;
still less do you do so if you have no counter ideas to
offer in exchange. This is the real reason why the
General came to grief. If you want to get the upper hand
of the ideologues it is fatal to have no trace of the philosopher in your composition.

Nevertheless, Primo di Rivera's government had some

solid achievements to its credit: the re-establishment of security, of public order, of credit and confidence, setting the nation to work again, which had a beneficial effect on the working classes; putting the financial house in order; construction of magnificent new roads; improved facilities for foreign tourists, and, abroad, the conquest of Alhucemas, the swift and effective pacification of Morocco.

A few years sufficed for the accomplishment of these various tasks. When they were completed the dictator found himself confronted by a void. He had not sense enough to depart in time. And so, like Don Quixote, he set out to give battle to all comers, indiscriminately. He piled on tolls and fines, he fell out with the press, abolished the High Court of Justice. And then at last he brought on a National Assembly, a caricature of Parliament, because he liked to act in conformity with the law.

The Dictator resurrects a parliament! This was the Empire run on liberal lines. There was something of the Napoleon III, that is to say a little off-handedness, a little diffidence, a certain condescending regard for his opponents' ideas, about this dictator, who gave the impression of not being quite easy in his mind about the lawfulness of his dictatorship. The opposition began to hold up their heads. Before long the army, the University and the world of business found themselves united in a common determination to checkmate the General's plans.

According to a century-old tradition in the Spanish Army, it was the artillery that headed the revolt.

To combat the opposition which he felt growing stronger every day, the dictator fell into one of the greatest errors a modern politician can commit, namely red tape-ism and centralization. It was simply suicidal.

Primo de Rivera, who had reckoned to put down separatism by abolishing provincial liberties, intensified it by denying the provinces the traditional autonomy which they demanded. He failed to act on that formula, apart from which there will never be domestic peace for Spain, namely a strong central government with a number of autonomous provinces about it.

This dearth of ideas, of principles, of teaching and of a political programme made it impossible for the dictator to stand up to the coalition which was taking shape against him. Some obscure tale of trouble about a petrol monopoly furnished his adversaries with a *casus belli* against him and his entourage. The agitation was started, the hunt was up and the hounds were in full cry at the heels of the dictator.

In the end, Primo di Rivera was undone by the machinations of his own people. The aristocracy dealt him the final blows. The Grandees, the King's entourage, the Court, all clamoured for his dismissal. They only saw his faults and were too ready to forget that in all probability they owed their lives to him.

In January, 1930, Primo left Spain for Paris, where he died suddenly two months later.

From a collaboration of the Crown and the Dictatorship, Spain might have witnessed the birth of a new order. Alfonzo XIII had never been wholeheartedly with the General. He now gave him up, to go back to the old

Spanish parliamentary machine, to that 'rota' system which though convenient, was artificial and impossible to restore. As the result of all these false moves, the Monarchy steadily lost ground. The premature collapse of the dictatorship had only left behind it a fresh crop of disorders. Three years after Primo's fall, Alfonzo XIII stood defenceless and alone against the triumphant forces of the revolution.

Its ultimate failure must not let us forget the good works wrought under the dictatorship of Primo de Rivera. It will leave us the memory of times that were happy, flourishing and honourable for Spain. As for the man himself, if he does not go down in history as a great man, he will certainly be regarded as a man of honour. But there's no playing the dictator with superfine manners and white kid gloves.

OLIVEIRA SALAZAR,
REFORMER OF PORTUGAL

AMONG all the countries of Europe, Portugal is the one which for thirty years had given evidence of the most unyielding anarchy.

It had been the first to experience the disorders attending the currency inflation which marked the end of the nineteenth century.

On the 1st February, 1908, an outrage carried out by the *carbonari* at the instigation of the Freemasons, cost King Carlos I and the Crown Prince Luis their lives. Both were assassinated before the very eyes of the noble-hearted Queen Amelia, a daughter of France.

This tragic event hurried on the decline of Portugal. King Manoel, who was a youth of eighteen when he succeeded to his father's throne, failed to reassert the authority of the Crown. In October, 1910, by a *coup d'état* carried out by the forces of Freemasonry, the Monarchy was overthrown and Portugal was proclaimed a Republic. From that time forward the country was given over to religious persecution, rioting, arbitrary arrests, assassinations and universal pillage.

During the war, a patriotic president of the Republic named Sidonio Paes made himself dictator with the support of the army and the approval of the populace. He immediately set his hand to some effective measures for bringing about the country's recovery. But at the end of 1918 he was assassinated by two men in the pay of the *carbonari*. Portugal relapsed into a period of disorder, a disorder that was aggravated by the Communist agitation.

In May, 1926, just when the country was nearing the last stages of political disintegration, the strong man arose. Marshal Gomez da Costa, who had fought brilliantly in Africa and on the French front, called on the army to rally to his support and, in company with General Carmona and General Cabecaola, set up a military triumvirate and marched on Lisbon. In a few days they gained control of the capital. They then issued a proclamation declaring that the country was determined to free itself from the tyranny of an irresponsible parliament and was about to create a system of national representation in which its interests would be duly observed.

This military dictatorship succeeded in re-establishing public order. For the rest its programme was at once too brief and too vague. It failed to secure governmental stability and proved unequal to arresting the financial collapse, leaving the country, in the middle of 1928, with no other course than an appeal to the League of Nations. The latter agreed to grant a loan, but only on condition that in future the whole of the finances of Portugal should come under its control. The country indignantly rejected the idea of such a humiliation.

It was at this juncture that someone called to mind Oliveira Salazar, an eminent, but retiring, Professor of

Law at the University of Coimbra. Barely forty years of age, Salazar was elected deputy in 1921 but said good-bye to Parliament after the first day's sitting. However, he accepted the portfolio of Finance in one of the ephemeral governments of 1926, and held it for three days.

On the 26th April, 1928, from purely patriotic motives, Salazar, yielding to the bitter reproaches of the government, undertook the Ministry of Finance. In doing so, he had laid it down as an absolutely essential condition, that he should have unrestricted control of expenditure, and that no other minister should be permitted to take a decision on any financial matter save with his concurrence.

His proclamation ran as follows: 'The rigid principles by which our common task will be guided show a clear determination to set in order, once for all, the financial and economic life of the nation. In this difficult task it is essential that I should possess the absolute but calm and serene confidence of the country. I know exactly what I want, and where I am going. I will, from time to time, as I proceed, give the country all the information necessary to enable it to take stock of the situation. The country may discuss, the country may study the matter, the country may make suggestions, but the country must obey when I give my orders.' He added that, personally, he had no desire for power, that he accepted it in order to render a service to Portugal, but that if anyone hindered him in carrying out his duty, he would at once return to Coimbra and his studies.

This was brief and to the point. The professor had

spoken like a real statesman. They did as they were told.

But, unlike the rest of them, Salazar had a definite political doctrine to put forward. He had been powerfully influenced by Charles Maurras.[1] He has stated that it is to him he owes the idea of strong government, the distinction between demophily and democracy. 'It is because we love the people', says Salazar, 'that we, for our part, do not want to have the governing power scattered over all their heads'.

Salazar's essential principles aim at the restoration of a code of justice and morality in the State based on Christianity and transcending the rights of the State. In short, the constant subordination of private interests to the interests of the nation as a whole is for him no platitude, but a living maxim.

Salazar's first task as president was to set the country's finances on a sound basis. To accomplish that end he contented himself with quite a simple programme, in marked contrast to the socialists who accompany every effort at economic restoration with a total destruction of the existing state of things, in order to make room for some new-fangled system as complex as it is problematic. But if Salazar's programme was simple, he took care that there should be no deviation from it, not so much as a hair's breadth, in its application.

[1] It behoves us here to point out the influence which French writers have had on the revolutionary movements of modern Europe. There is Mussolini. He too, is not unacquainted with the ideas of Charles Maurras. Lenin was enlightened by Georges Sorel's *Reflections on Violence*. The Young Turks borrowed the notion of a Turkey distinct from the Arab world and separated from Islam, from Léon Cahun's *Introduction to the History of Asia*. Finally Hitler's racial ideas come straight out of Gobineau.

When he assumed his task, Salazar found himself confronted by the most chaotic financial muddle in Europe. In two years from then he succeeded, by means of a strict readjustment of income and expenditure, in balancing the budget. If he put a big increase on some of the duties, he also contrived, by a more equitable distribution of the liability, to recover the amount he needed without imposing an impossible burden on the taxpayer. The average scale of taxation in Portugal is definitely less than it is in France, or in Great Britain. In all matters concerned with expenditure, salaries, pensions, subsidies and so forth, the dictator's sanction is a *sine qua non*.

When Salazar has any communication to make to his fellow-citizens it is nearly always to remind them that the work before them calls for sacrifice, but that the sacrifice will safeguard the future of Portugal and of their children. The members of the Government, and of the Public Services, set a salutary example by the simplicity of their lives. With them, unselfishness is raised to the rank of a guiding principle in State affairs.

In consequence of these rules of strict economy, Portugal, for the past seven years, has been able to carry on a very extensive and well co-ordinated scheme of national improvement. The results have been brilliant. The whole of the country's road system has been reconstructed and developed, schools, hospitals, dispensaries have been built, the Navy has been reconditioned and the Army reorganized. For the first time in its history, the country honours all its signatures, and has thus regained the confidence of the foreigner. Finally in the domain of public expenditure, a clean sweep has been made of the graft, wastage and bribery which in former times sapped the life-blood of the humblest enterprise.

The formation of trade guilds is under consideration with the object of improving the relations between capital and labour.

With the support of a Minister of Justice, M. Corbal, who like most of the dictator's collaborators, is a young man, Salazar brought a bill before the National Assembly condemning Freemasonry and all secret societies. It went through without a division.

Freemasonry is condemned because it is inimical to those principles of Christian justice which are upheld by the government and are indissolubly interwoven with Portuguese traditions; because its purposes have nothing in common with those of the nation; because it restricts the free and independent action of the government and regards its sectarian interests as of greater importance than the interests of the nation, of which it is as regardless as it is of individual merit, its object, as its statutes declare, being to secure office for its adherents; and lastly, because in Portugal, it was primarily responsible for the revolutionary disorders which, for twenty years, plunged the country into bankruptcy and stained its annals with blood.

M. Salazar and his colleagues have virtually the solid backing of their fellow-countrymen behind them. The two opposing minorities are, on the Right, some of the younger university people, who would like a government that would think more of national prestige and who criticize the existing régime for the modesty of its pretensions. On the Left, the Freemasons and the anticlericals have not laid down their arms. But against the triumphant success, material and moral, of Oliveira Salazar's rule, the opposition makes but a feeble and ineffective display. It is a dictatorship that has secured its hold on the country without recourse to force, by no other means than the straightforward honesty of its methods, and by the prosperity, the real prosperity and activity which it succeeded in imparting to Portugal at the very time when all the other nations of the world were complaining of the severity of the crisis. It was the most upright, the wisest and the most moderate in Europe, and, at the same time, one of the strongest and one of the most persevering in pursuing the practical application of its principles.

The utter failure in September last of the most recent attempt to overthrow it, affords pretty conclusive evidence that it is far from nearing its end.

It is commonly said that we have got a 'Republic of Professors' and the people who say it clearly do not like it. Well, Portugal has a Dictatorship of Professors, and finds it excellent. How multifarious the world is; how plastic!

HITLER

THE latest comer to the ranks of European dictators is not the one the nature of whose personality and task are the most easy to understand. No other man of our times has been the subject of interpretations at once so varied and so numerous. Every time he took a step forward, it was prophesied that his fall was at hand. It is true that the disappearance of Benito Mussolini had also been long predicted as imminent. In spite of this, Hitler, in a few years, has become not only master of Germany, but one of the two or three men who hold the fate of Europe in the palm of their hand.

As most people know, Adolf Hitler was not by birth a German citizen. He first saw the day in 1889, at Braunau-am-Inn, a tiny market town whose inhabitants, as Hitler himself has told us, though politically Austrians, are Bavarians by race. It is situated on the frontier of those two Germanic states, Germany and Austria, and to unite them into a single Empire the future Chancellor of the Reich was one day to regard as his primary task. His father was an employee in the customs service, and he wanted his son to be a civil servant. But the son declined and declared that he wished to become a painter. He was then a boy of twelve. A year later, the father died, and Adolf Hitler left his school for the Academy of Fine Arts at Vienna.

After his mother's death, he continued to live on there for several years, having found out that, though his vocation as a painter was not perhaps one of the deepest, he had an undeniable leaning towards architecture. He stopped on for five years in Vienna, five years of pretty grinding poverty, during which he doggedly pursued his studies, working as a day-labourer the while, and reading any and every book he could lay hands on. All his ideas, he tells us, were formed at this time, and it was now, too, that he learnt to understand men. Above all, it was now that he came to hate the Hapsburg monarchy, and now that he conceived his social ideas, his distrust of social-democracy and Marxism, and his violent anti-Semitism.

In 1912, Adolf Hitler left Vienna for Munich, a city of which he was particularly fond and where, if only on account of the Bavarian dialect, he felt much more at home than in the Austro-Hungarian capital. He began to take up a line of politics hostile to the Austro-German alliance which, according to him, was bound to end in catastrophe, and he affirmed that the first task that ought to claim attention was the destruction of Marxism. When the war broke out, he succeeded in enlisting in a Bavarian regiment.

He went through the war with enthusiasm. 'There began for me then,' he afterwards wrote, 'as for every German, the most unforgettable, and the sublimest days of my earthly existence'. He was wounded and in hospital when, in 1918, he learnt simultaneously of the armistice and the revolution. He had nearly lost his eyesight and, though spared that disaster, he was obliged to give up his drawing. He made a solemn vow that he would devote his life to the welfare of his country.

Having been ordered (for he was not yet out of the army) to conduct an inquiry into certain revolutionary activities in his regiment, he was brought into contact with a political association which had just been formed calling itself the 'German Labour Party'. Not long afterwards he received, without in any way soliciting it, a card informing him that he had been enrolled as a member. Somewhat taken aback at this strange method of securing adherents, he went to one of the committee-meetings and was staggered at its old-fashioned, circumlocutionary methods. Then he had an idea. He said to himself that, if he wanted to achieve anything, the right way was not to go and join some immense organization, but to throw in his lot with some little, unknown body which he could do what he liked with, and soon become its leader. So he decided to take the step. He became a member of the German Labour Party and his ticket of membership was No. 7. That was in 1919, and it is true that, up till then, the party had only consisted of six members.

Needless to say that at first the meetings of this embryonic and rather comical little imitation of a political group, which aimed at nothing less than the reconstitution of the German Empire in all its might and majesty, passed entirely unnoticed. One day, however, they managed to get as many as a hundred and eleven people together — forty less than Mussolini collected for the first political meeting of the Fascists. For the first time Hitler spoke in public. In half an hour his auditors were wild with enthusiasm. Hitler had proved himself a great orator. In 1920, at Munich, he held the first great meeting of the German National Socialist Labour Party (such was the new name it had adopted). It was an enormous success.

Little by little, the association added to its numbers. The campaign was directed simultaneously against three foes: Marxism, the Jews and the Versailles Treaty. There was yet another enemy to contend with: separatism. Too little importance has been attached by the French to German separatist tendencies. One has but to glance through the pages of *Mein Kampf* to see how keen was the hostility entertained in certain quarters towards Prussia and the bare notion of a Reich. It is by no means certain that Hitler himself was not in touch with the separatists of Bavaria and the Rhineland. At all events, Bavarian independence was a theme dear to many in his party. There was even some talk of constituting a new State uniting Bavaria with Austria. It appeared to offer a better chance of success than the *Anschluss*. To what extent Hitler identified himself with these divers tendencies he refrains from telling us. What, however, is beyond dispute is that he soon took up arms against 'parliamentarism' in any shape or form, and conceived the ideal of a totalitarian and absolutely indivisible Reich. But his assurance that this conception had always been with him we should do well to treat with some reserve.

Hitler owed it to his extraordinary gifts of oratory that he was able to bring together audiences of ever-increasing magnitude, and that, despite attacks by the Socialists, who were beginning to realize how strong a force was wielded by this group which yesterday no one had ever heard of. He carried on his propaganda without concealment and altogether refused to have anything to do with secret society methods. Hitler has always stoutly denied that he was in any way mixed up with the political murders which stain the annals of post-war Germany, although the perpetrators have included in their ranks many men who ardently sympathized with the National Socialist Party, even if they did not belong to it. Thus Ernst von Salomon, the writer, who was mixed up with Rathenau's assassination, was, at all events for a time, a convinced Hitlerian.

Organized in broad daylight, National-Socialism had its colours, its orchestra (no German party without its band! No speech by Hitler without the Big Drum!) and its shock-troops who were soon to become famous. Before long they had their uniform — the brown shirt — and their insignia, the Swastika, which represents the sun, and which Germany has taken from the East. In 1922, Hitler bought up a little weekly paper, the *Volkische Beobachter* which the following year he turned into a daily.

After the French occupation of the Ruhr, effected with an absence of resistance that shows to what depths of helplessness the Reich had sunk, many Germans considered that only some radical transformation which should make a clean sweep of the post-war political system and of the republican constitution of Weimar could ever bring back greatness to their country.

Hitler thought the moment had arrived. He attempted a *putsch*, with Ludendorff to back him, and the result was the abortive revolution of the 8th November, 1923, in which eighteen of his followers, the earliest 'martyrs' of the Nazi movement lost their lives, shot down outside the Feldherrenhalle at Munich. To their memory *Mein Kampf* was dedicated. After a long trial, in which he defended the cause of his party and the Reich, he was found guilty on the 1st April, 1924, and put into prison at Landsberg-am-Lecht.

There, at last, he found repose. He availed himself of it to put his ideas in order and set them down in a book, his celebrated *Mein Kampf* (My Struggle) which is, as it were, the Koran of Nazi-ism and still enjoys a remarkable success.

It is perhaps rather difficult for a Frenchman to understand this book. An initial misunderstanding vitiates every perusal of *Mein Kampf*. We search it for a political and social programme, and we find it, page upon page of it. The most diverse questions — education, campaign against venereal disease, history, naturalization — all are touched on in this huge volume with its seven hundred pages, while, at the same time, Hitler gives an account of his own intellectual evolution. But there is no escaping the conclusion that the essence of the book is not in these things. In the mind of its author, as in the minds of millions of its readers, *Mein Kampf* is first and foremost the sacred book of a religion, the Gospel of National-Socialism, or, to speak more correctly, of race-worship.

The real Hitler did not exist before those years of hardship in Vienna, where he simultaneously discovered the dangers of Marxism and of Jewish World-Ascendancy. His real birth as a man of action dates from the day on which he discovered ethnology. It is in this department that a Frenchman is bound to find *Mein Kampf* singularly inadequate, singularly elementary. If we had to judge these fighting books by the same canons as we judge works of the mind, it is certain that the National Socialist Bible would not bear a moment's examination. The most puerile absurdities mingle with the most dubious scientific hypotheses, all couched in language whose pedantry, though it take one's breath away, probably contributed in large measure to the book's success with German readers.

In Hitler's eyes, it is the Aryans who have given to civilization its enduring quality, the civilization without which no nation can escape extinction, and of which traces are to be found even in modern Japan. And among the Aryans, the purest, the genuine heirs of Hellenism (Hitler, like all Germans, loves to bring in the Greeks) are the Teutons. The Germanic races have been entrusted with a sacred mission, which they have not as yet completely fulfilled, by reason of their internal divisions and certain long-standing political errors. Nevertheless, wheresoever on the earth the Germanic race has presented itself, there the world is invited to admire its greatness and the beauty of the results it has achieved. Thus Russia, an essentially barbarian country, only succeeded in becoming more or less a nation, by reason of the Germanic elements which it contained and to which it always left the guidance of the State. The greatest Russian ruler was Catherine II, a German princess.

Unfortunately, over against the ever-growing glory of this Helleno-Germanic civilization, the Jews have raised their heads. Hitler's references to the Jews are always characterized by the deepest hatred and a complete absence of the critical spirit. What, we may ask, are his real ideas on this vital subject? We cannot confidently say that we know what they are. Nor is the mysterious anti-Semitic policy of the Third Reich calculated to enlighten us. The ideas which the author of *Mein Kampf* seems to adumbrate regarding the development of the Jewish nation throughout the world are so clumsy that we cannot help wondering whether they are not to be regarded as gaudy mythical pictures deliberately intended to stir the crowd, the rank and file of the fighting forces, to action, rather than as the reasoned conclusions of a sincere and sober mind.

For Hitler, the famous *Protocoles des Sages de Sion* (that Messianic essay, which some have held to be nothing less than a work of the *agent-provocateur* order, manufactured by the Tzarist police on the pattern of a French pamphlet against Napoleon III) present, in all essentials, the Jewish plan for the conquest and enslavement of the world. He speaks of the Jews not merely as a danger for the whole of Western civilization, but as a mysterious secret society that never loses sight of its aim or of the means to attain it, an elaborate organization which he is ready and eager to expose and which is apparently directed by an invisible High Command in America, England or Jerusalem. Nor can it be denied that to embody an enemy in a certain group of persons and to imagine the existence of an all-powerful secret society is excellent propaganda. As a counterblast to Hitler's Jewish Council, the Marxists bring forward their

Comité des Forges, a conspiracy of armament manufacturers. There is nothing like a myth to rouse the fanaticism of the masses, and secure their blind devotion.

The conflict between these great forces, Germanism and Semitism, fills *Mein Kampf* with considerations which, though often vague, are always compelling, and which have no doubt done far more for the success of the book than the few lucid pages which may here and there be found in it. It is those quasi-metaphysical considerations, wherein we recognize distorted versions of the doctrines of Nietzsche and Gobineau, which account for most of Hitler's reactions to the essential problems by which the German nation is confronted.

The first, which concerns those Germans who are politically outside the Empire, is the union under one flag and in one spirit, with everything and everybody that is German, Austria first of all. The Jews, he declared, were predominant in the Hapsburg Monarchy, and that is why he hates the older dynasties. For two centuries, he says, they have always failed in their essential duties to the German race. As for the other races of German blood and German speech, Hitler is not disposed to commit himself, and his ideas have suddenly and singularly taken on an opportunism in marked contrast to the mysticism which coloured their beginning. Thus he explicitly condemns the claims which some Germans persist in putting forward to that part of the Tyrol which is under Italian rule. The outstanding object is to join up with Austria. There must be no risk of a misunderstanding with Italy, of whom Germany might stand in need (besides, Hitler declares himself an admirer of

Mussolini) for the sake of the two hundred thousand or
so Germans of the Trentino, of whom he has no very
high opinion. People, he says, who keep their gaze
fixed on the Tyrol and nothing else, little dream that
they are playing into the hands of the Jews and of France.
It is true that Italy has stood in the way of German
development, but then, since the war, by whom has not
Germany been despoiled? That is no reason for holding
aloof from every country in Europe. As for those who
favour an alliance with France, Hitler reminds them
en passant that France robbed them of Alsace-Lorraine.

France (as we know, the French translation of *Mein
Kampf* was banned) remains the chief obstacle to Germany's aspirations. And Hitler makes no attempt to
deny that, sooner or later, there will have to be a reckoning with France. 'These results,' he says, 'will not be
attained by praying to God, nor by speeches, nor by
negotiations at Geneva. They will be attained by war
and bloodshed.' France, indeed, is Germany's inveterate
foe. England, says Hitler, in one of the most intelligent
chapters in his book, does not want any Continental
power to be strong enough to stand up to her. So her
aim is to pit France against Germany; with the corollary
that, if and when it seems expedient, she will pit Germany
against France. France's aim, on the other hand, is to
bring about the disappearance of Germany as a power
in politics by cutting her up into little pieces. That is
why an understanding is possible with England, but not
with France.

And, so as to make his detailed policy square with the
National-Socialist creed, Hitler goes on to add that

France is not fit to live in a world in which racial purity is essential. France indeed, who went to the length of using black troops to guard the Rhine, as well as employing them for service in the field, is rapidly losing her racial integrity by her continual absorption of alien races. From the Congo to Alsace, he says, we may see the gradual formation of a vast Negro-French Empire, which will become increasingly impure as time goes on. That, it is the duty of civilization to prevent.

In this way it will be possible to establish German supremacy (or the Third Reich, as it quickly came to be designated) over a regenerate universe.

We are tempted to laugh at this grotesque line of argument, these rash assertions, these wild inventions. Nevertheless, it is to them that Hitler owes his power. And that, perhaps, is the gravest part of it all, for it is nothing less than the mystery of that indefinable something which is fermenting in the German brain.

At the time Hitler came out of prison he was much less known in France than the chief of the National Conservatives, one of Germany's captains of industry, Hugenberg. In 1919, Hugenberg, the leading figure in the metallurgical world in Germany, had about a hundred deputies in the Reichstag at his beck and call. In 1932, his followers did not number more than fifty. Between these two dates, the Hitlerian movement had progressed at his expense. However, Hugenberg still wielded a great deal of influence, thanks to the control he exercised over the public press and to the Cinematograph Society which Krupp had brought into being during the war. Between Hugenberg, who financed and

really controlled the Steel Helmets, and Hitler, the
Master of the National-Socialist Storm Troops, rivalry
was inevitable. It was long, and marked by alternate
rapprochements and mistrust. It continued until Hitler
definitely got the power into his own hands.

This is not the place to recount all the numerous
episodes of the struggle. Suffice it to recall that the Hitler
movement, backed up by the brown-shirt legions, continued to grow, while the world at large refused to believe that a personage so ridiculous could possibly become
master of Germany. Others considered that he was just
the ordinary sort of popular agitator, that his importance
had been greatly exaggerated. They held that he lacked
resolution, that he was a sick man, and that it was now
too late for him to attempt a march on Berlin. As a
matter of fact he was very calculating and cunning and
was paving his way in perfect security, in secret accord
with what in Germany have always been known as the
'spheres'. On the 30th January, 1933, Hitler was sent
for by the aged Marshal von Hindenburg and requested
to form a government. He thus became Chancellor of
the Reich ten years after the failure of his *putsch* in 1923.
His friend Goering, one of the outstanding personalities
of the party, was Minister of Police in the Reich.
Hugenberg's Nationalists had the departments of Finance
Commerce, Industry, Public Works, and Foreign Affairs.
The Vice-Chancellor, the adroit von Papen, was the
liaison officer between the two groups.

This alliance with the old Right could not last. It
soon became obvious to everyone that the various offices
would be united in the hands of Hitler and his two lieu-

tenants, Goering and the romantic Goebbels, a recruit from Socialism, the most 'advanced' theorist of the group, and the most ardent anti-Semite.

In 1933, after failing, in spite of a raging, tearing campaign, to secure the presidency of the Reich, Hitler one night — the 30th June, 1934 — proceeded to the purgation of his party, as such purges had been carried out during the revolution. On that tragic night, General von Schleicher and his wife and Roehm, head of the S.Z. were assassinated. People were reminded at once of the 'gangsters' of Chicago and the murder of Sejanus. Soon afterwards, on the 2nd August, 1934, and twenty years after the declaration of war, the aged Marshal von Hindenburg passed away. Becoming at once President and Chancellor of the Reich, Hitler was henceforth the legal master of Germany and none dared openly attack him.

Such an astounding rise to fortune would have been impossible without the help and goodwill of a nation, in this case a nation susceptible beyond all others to the obscure influences of instinct and poetry.

It is certain that Hitler owes an enormous debt to his 'legend'. His foes help to build it up by relating impossible stories about him, saying that the 'ex-house-painter' is a madman, an imbecile, and accusing him of practising unnatural vices; while his friends contribute their quota by their ceaseless panegyrics of his genius. Nor must it by any means be overlooked that the Hitlerian party have encompassed the gods of their worship with a complete cycle or system of music which has made Germany drunk with enthusiasm.

Without the songs of the Storm Troops, where would Hitlerism be? One ought to have heard what went on during the 1933 elections, the songs, the hymns, the dramatic performances, the try-out of a radiophonic art in which noise and music were of more importance than the words, speeches punctuated by thumps on the big drum — one ought to have heard all this in order to realize the degree of frenzy to which massed German crowds can attain. Hitler and Goebbels are both great orators. Goebbels always speaks in a very high key. In a voice that never wearies and with an almost preter-human energy, he foretells a great social upheaval and the rebuilding of the fabric of German greatness. Hitler begins his speeches on an almost ordinary pitch; after a while, his voice grows hoarse and louder, losing all semblance of human tone, and he speaks on and on like one inebriated with the sound of his own words, holding his listeners in thrall, as by a sort of barbaric incantation. The word 'Germany' recurs like a refrain in every ten sentences of these interminable harangues. From time to time, the orchestra is called in, to add to the effect; so are the immense choirs who celebrate the heroes slain by the French, like Horst Wessel, who was eaten up with vice, and Schlageter, who was probably a spy, the pair who are held up to admiration as the Harmodius and Aristogiton of Germany, the Castor and Pollux of the Third Reich. An election campaign takes to the scenic accompaniments of one of Wagner's fabulous music-dramas.

These chants, with their slow and tragic rhythm, are sometimes not without a beauty of their own. With the romance of forget-me-nots and rustic fountains they mingle the uncouth arrogance of later times.

O dark hair'd daughter — wherefore weepest thou so sorely?
A young officer of Hitler's battalion hath stol'n my heart away.

There went a-marching by a regiment of the Oberland — a regiment of horse, a regiment of foot . . .

Or again there is the Hymn to those who fell on the 9th November:

In Munich many were the Fallen — Many were they that fell in Munich — They fell by the Felderenhalle — it was there that the bullets struck them down.

Then there are the most famous patriotic hymns of New Germany:

The mountaineer cometh down to the plain, the peasant looseneth the grip of his rugged hands upon the plough, the young folk refuse to be bondslaves to the base; and from the Alps right down to the sea the tempests of Germany echo the song that bringeth fear to the heart of Juda; the chains are breaking in sunder and the Month of May looketh down with smiles upon us. Arise, O Germany! The hour of thy deliverance hath sounded!

And the Song which sings of Horst Wessel and '*the comrades, slain by the Reds and by the forces of Reaction, who march on, in the spirit, in our ranks.*' Without music, Germany would follow no one.

To such an extent has Goebbels realized the importance of charming eye and ear that he has organized mighty festivals, which defy every canon of taste, and extol the grandeur of the new régime.

In *Mein Kampf*, Hitler has some hard things to say about those racial fanatics who would fain go back to Wotan and Walhalla, who bedeck themselves with false beards, sneer at Christianity and, by distracting men's minds from the essential work in hand, do but further the aims of the Jews. But, since then, it cannot be denied that his ideas have undergone a change. The May Day celebrations bring back the orgies of Walpurgis, round mighty bonfires leap and dance young men and maidens, drunk with music. The Neo-Pagan movement, condemned by Bishop and by Pastor, is daily growing in importance. The magic and sorcery of Old Germany were brought into play to help de-Christianize the country and to bring it back to what it was in the days before St. Boniface. Here, again, comes into play the German love for the dark and mysterious forces of nature, a romanticism 'of the earth, earthy', as Count Keyserling might put it, and worlds away from the spirit of France.

All this process of bewitchment was accompanied by very definite action. It is needless to recall how the Socialists have been reduced to silence, how the recalcitrants are shut up for months on end in concentration camps and, in particular, how, in 1933, a large number of Jews were induced to quit Germany *en masse*. It seems, however, that, as often as not, they have left it as socialists much rather than as Jews. Furthermore, taking his cue from certain American States, and because he liked to think he was doing something scientific — he has always liked to imagine himself something of a scientist — Hitler caused a measure to be passed making sterilization compulsory in the case of certain afflicted people. This brought him into conflict with the Church.

For, like every other dictator, he was bound to come

up against the religious problem before long. By birth he is a Catholic, and, as for the Lutheran Church, he wanted to organize that under the supreme headship of a bishop vowed to his allegiance. Then he rated the Catholics, accusing them of not submitting to his leadership with becoming resignation. The conception of a Glorified State, which is the head and front of his system, the sterilization law to which we have just referred, the objections taken by him to certain Catholic personages, the Neo-Pagan manifestations, the massacres of the 30th June were bound to revolt Catholic Germany. The Bishops, who had been rather hesitating in their condemnation of Hitler and his methods before his triumph, met at Fulda in July, 1935, and solemnly renewed their anathema. Will the Fürher shatter himself 'upon this rock' or will he go to Canossa?

However, it must be recognized that, from the political point of view, Hitler, succeeding as he did to the task of one of the most astute and gifted of German statesmen, namely Stresemann, displayed much greater address than he had been credited with. His studied insolence, his audacities, his 'sharp practices' have stood him and his country in good stead. One after another, he is obliterating the last traces of the defeat, it being understood that his movement springs from the conviction, which, from the beginning, was strongly held by the Germans, that their defeat was something undeserved, a sort of misdeal at the hands of Fate. As a result of his understandings with foreign countries and especially with England, he has achieved the task of national regeneration to which all his efforts have been devoted.

There are many features in this Hitlerian movement which are still shrouded in mystery. Some people have described it as a second Reformation, a second uprising of the 'Teutonic Man'. On the national and political plane, the objects aimed at are openly stated, and the results are not in doubt. It is on the social plane that uncertainty begins. It is not very clear what Hitler is going to do with his vast armies of unemployed who are now assembling in labour camps. All we know is that he is training them for war. As against all this, there is not the smallest doubt that among his troops he has a large number of communists compelled to hide convictions that may still be lively and sincere. Supposing some great upheaval takes place, what will become of these troops? And what will become of Germany?

And then, lastly, to come to the mystical and religious plane, no one knows as yet how Hitler will manage to settle matters with the various Christian denominations to whom he is always giving manifold causes of offence.

We have been told by one who has travelled a good deal in Germany where he has conversed very freely with Germans of all sorts and heard them expound their divers views, sometimes not unmingled with severe criticism of the new régime, that on one occasion he put the following question to an avowed communist:

'What,' he said, 'ought we to think of Hitler?'

'There's no denying Hitler's personality,' was the other's prompt reply.

The French people, who pay a willing tribute to Mussolini, are not wholly convinced of the truth of that statement. Some people have given them to understand that Germany's hero is a puppet and they have given credence to the statement. Certainly a perusal of *Mein Kampf* is — if we except the pages which treat of foreign policy — well calculated to disappoint. And we do not say that Hitler is an intelligent man in the sense we usually apply to the word. But in a few years, he has succeeded in winning for himself a position above all others, a position which sometimes makes us think of Bonaparte. Perhaps in a sense the man will always elude us, but this much is certain: it is on him that all the hopes of the Germany that was vanquished in 1918 are centred. Our socialists are all at sea about him. Every step forward that he took, they said his fall was imminent. He mirrors too faithfully certain aspects of his country, for that fall, even if it occurs, to be of much account. But the important thing is to know him, not to suffer ourselves to be misled by his rudimentary and inchoate ideas. Beneath a very elementary philosopher, there leaps to the eye a politician who knows what he wants and whose position makes him, however vehemently he may declare and believe himself the contrary, France's most formidable antagonist.

CONCLUSION

CONCLUSION

WHETHER one wants, or whether one fears, a dictator, it seems to us that this review, incomplete though it be, should enable every man to judge for himself.

From demagogy to tyranny is but a single step, whether the strong man is born of a reaction against the forces of disorder, or whether he imposes revolutionary changes in which the moderates and the conservatives have to suffer.

'The wise men of old, who were well worth the new ones,' knew that perfectly well. In the last century, being impressed with the success of Napoleon III, they taught that socialism led to imperialism. But socialism is the perfect expression of democracy. Not indeed its final expression, for nothing ever ends. We revolve eternally in cycles. Whatever implies constraint in the social organism entails the disappearance of political freedom and postulates a power with which no argument is possible.

If anarchy engenders Caesars because order is an elementary necessity of societies, communism also produces other Caesars, because it orders everything.

We have only to speak of 'regulated economy' to infer the existence of a supreme regulator. So it is, then, the 'too much' and the 'not enough' that are both productive of dictators.

Whether they be of the Right or of the Left, and they are usually the latter, they carry with them a large measure of uncertainty. It is desirable to be sparing of them, desirable, that is, not to have need of them, or not to drift into them unwittingly.

Eckermann once asked Goethe if the human race would ever see the end of war. ''Yes,' answered the sage of Weimar, 'provided that governments are always intelligent and the governed always reasonable.' We will say the same of dictators. We can do without them on the same condition. But good governments are rare. And Voltaire said that the bulk of the human race always were, and always would be, imbeciles.

INDEX

INDEX

INDEX

Danton, 94-6
Diaz, Porfirio, 132-3
Diderot, 86, 89, 91
Doubasov, General, 172
Doumergue, Gaston, 21

ECKERMANN, 262
Elba, 110
Elluari, 154
Enghien, Duc d', 108

FACTA, SIGNOR, 222
Falkenhayn, General, 198
Ferdinand VII, 131, 135
Flahaut, General de, 117
Flores, Juan, 147, 154
Fouché, 98
Fouquet, 80
Francia, 154, 155
Franklin, Benjamin, 87
Frederick II of Prussia, 85, 88-90
Fronde, The, 80-82

GAMARRA, 157
Gaxotte, Pierre, 85
Gengis Khan, 197
Giolitti, 206, 218
Gobineau, 248
Goebbels, 252-4
Goering, 251, 252
Goethe, 262
Gomez, Juan Vicente, 145
Gonsalez, General, 132
Gorki, 182
Gouraud, General, 198
Guatimozin, 126-7
Guesde, Jules, 173
Guibert, Comte de, 102
Guiscard, Robert, 144

HAMPDEN, JOHN, 62
Harmodius, 24
Henri IV, 69, 73
Hidalgo, Miguel, 128-130
Hipparchus, 25
Hippias, 25
Hitler, Adolf, not a German by birth, 240; at Vienna, 241; his war service, 241; a great orator, 243; abortive attempt at revolution, 244; is imprisoned, 245; writes *Mein Kampf*, 245; his race worship, 246; becomes Chancellor, 251; the night of June 30th, 1934, 252; becomes President, 252; France's chief antagonist, 258

HÉBERT, 96-7
Helvetius, Madame, 105
Herbois, Collot d', 97
Hindenburg, Marshal von, 251, 252
Hortense, Queen, 114, 115, 117
Hugenberg, 250
Hugo, Victor, 101, 113, 119

INDIA COMPANY, THE, 98
Ioudenitch, General, 183
Iturbide, Colonel, 131

JÉRÔME, KING, 117
John VI, Emperor and King of Brazil and Portugal, 161, 162
Joinville, Prince de, 115
Joseph II, of Hungary, 85, 88, 89, 91
Juarez, Benito, 131
Jugurtha, 38

KAMENEV, 190, 191
Kaplan, Dora, 187
Kerensky, 174-7, 179
Keyserling, Count, 255
Kornilov, General, 177

LAFUENTE, 157
Lebrun, 107
Lenin, founds the Militant Union, 169; organizes revolution, 172; his view of the war, 173; granted a free passage through German territory to Russia, 176; charged with high treason he flees to Finland, 176; returns secretly to Russia, 177; supports the treaty of Brest-Litovsk, 181; his work as dictator, 180 *et seq.*
Lopez, Antonio, 156
—— Solano, 156
Louis XI, 155
—— XIII, 57, 71, 72, 79, 81
—— XIV, 80, 86, 87, 158
—— XV, 62, 86, 90, 101, 107
—— XVIII, 110
—— of Holland, 112, 113
Louis-Philippe, 113
Louvois, 84
Ludendorff, 244
Luçon, Bishop of, 74
Luis, Crown Prince of Portugal, 233
Luxemburg, Rosa, 182
Lycurgus, 19

INDEX